THE
GOOD NEWS
WE PREACH
Gospel Truth in Modern China

Edited by
Qiangwei and Hannah Nation

CHINA PARTNERSHIP

TABLE OF CONTENTS

Preface by Hannah Nation   1

Introduction: The Gospel We Share
by Bryan Chapell   3

1. The Gospel Gives Us Union with Christ
   by James Miao   15

2. The Gospel Restores Intimacy With God   41
   by James Qin

3. The Gospel of Grace Alone by Li Ye   63

4. The Gospel Restores the Order of God
   by Brian Li   83

Endnotes   109

About the Editors   113

Preface

What does gospel partnership look like among global churches of the 21st century? Certainly it looks like many things, but I am convinced one of the more distinct features of the future of missional partnership is to be found in the written word. Christians have long been people of the word; now in our digital age, that importance has only increased. We now have unprecedented access to the church in other global contexts, even in places like China. As such, we live in a time in which we must carefully consider how to pursue partnership—and fellowship—through the written word.

The story behind this small volume highlights the possibilities which lie before us. When China Partnership published its first book *Grace to the City*, based on a series of conference talks delivered by Chinese house church pastors in 2017, Bryan Chapell graciously contributed a foreword. That foreword was shared with Qiangwei, a Chinese writer and editor who used a translated version to solicit essays written in response by dozens of leading house church pastors across China. Those essays were then turned into the first book produced by the Grace to City gospel movement in Chinese, *The Gospel We Preach*. And now in this book we have selected a few of these chapters to translate to English, completing a conversation that began in 2017. In a sense, this book is part of an ongoing, living conversation between the American church and the Chinese church—a partnership of mutual edification through the written word.

You are actively partnering with the Chinese house church simply by reading this book and by letting the reflections of your Chinese brothers encourage you in your walk with Christ. Though they cannot be in the same room with you today, taking the time to learn from these pastors contributes to the ongoing conversation. You stand with them and cheer them on by submitting yourselves to their teaching on the nature of the gospel.

These chapters represent some of the key themes Grace to City is reflecting on: the nature of salvation and how we are transformed in Christ; the nature of our union and intimacy with Christ; how to effectively disciple; and the metanarrative of redemption. While these themes are important for China, a society that has had their worldview overturned and is trying to answer life's most basic questions about reality, who would say these matters aren't also of vital importance to us in the Western church? As such, many things in this book will feel familiar. But we hope that hearing from a church that is currently experiencing a new cultural engagement with the gospel will refresh your understanding of and worship of Jesus Christ.

Hannah Nation
September 2021

Introduction:
The Gospel We Share

Bryan Chapell

When my wife's grandmother was a child, she dreamed of being a missionary to China. When she was a young woman, she attended The Bible Institute of Los Angeles to gain the knowledge and skills to be a missionary to China. When she married a ministry student with a mutual love for the gospel, they prepared for life as missionaries in China – until the medical diagnoses that disqualified them from mission service.

The young couple turned to ministry in the United States. The young pastor served a number of rural churches in the heartland of this country. The young wife faithfully supported his work, and even preached the last sermon he had written when a weak heart condition suddenly claimed the young preacher's life. The tragedy deepened the young woman's sense of availability and calling for missionary service. She dreamed of mission in China, and read everything she could about its people, history, and gospel influence, until the stroke that disabled her for the rest of her life.

The disability did not damage her prayers. The rest of her life she read, wrote, and prayed about the Chinese people that she had never met but loved for Christ's sake. So much was China in her thoughts and prayers, when age and dementia began to cloud her thoughts, she would tell her grandchildren of mission work she had done in the land she had actually never visited.

Her children and grandchildren would smile and wink at each other, knowing her memories were flawed, but I do not believe the angels laughed. They knew that her prayers had been her work, and that the gospel she loved had advanced beyond human accounting by the way that she had united her heart with the hearts of the Chinese people for Christ's sake.

Her prayers reach even to this day and to my life, as multiple trips to China have enabled me to unite my heart with dear Chinese brothers and sisters for Christ's sake. These faithful and courageous believers have not only helped me fulfill an ancestor's prayers by receiving the gospel message from me, they have also taught me more of the strength and hope of the Gospel.

As they live and love the truths of Scripture despite the difficulties and pressures of present day China, I learn that the prayers of a woman who faced tragedy all of her adult life are still bringing fruit in a distant nation and in my heart. I learn from my Chinese brothers and sisters that the Gospel we share is more powerful, precious, and good than history can tell or humans can estimate. This Gospel is not limited by time, ethnicities, or national boundaries. It is not the possession of any one people, culture, or generation. It is not stopped by personal tragedy; it cannot be suppressed by national persecution.

The Gospel is the unstoppable steel locomotive of God's purpose that rolls through history and hearts with the message of Christ's eternal mercy, pardon, and love to set free the souls of all who seek Him. All believers unite in this "good news" for mutual love, learning and support. We learn more of the Gospel's depth and richness when we hear it from those of other cultures who are expressing its truths from contexts presently unfamiliar to us. Our learning is not merely for the expansion of our minds. When we listen with humility and eagerness to Christian leaders of other cultures, we are preparing our hearts and future generations with the breadth of Christian truth and experience that are necessary to address the scope of spiritual challenges sure to come until Christ returns.

Out of my respect for the prayers of my ancestor, I now offer this brief essay on the nature of the Gospel for my Chinese brothers and sisters. Then, out of respect for the able and faithful scholars who write from a Chinese perspective, I will read with humility and eagerness of that same Gospel, knowing that they are helping to prepare me for the calling still ahead that we must face together for Christ's sake.

1. The Gospel Is Good News

Now I would remind you, brothers, of the gospel I preached to you, which you received, in which you stand, and by which you are being saved... For I delivered to you as of first importance what I also received: that Christ died for our sins in accordance with the Scriptures, that he was buried, that he was raised on the third day in accordance with the Scriptures. — 1 Corinthians 15:1–4

The word, "gospel," means "good news" in the language used in Biblical times. The Apostle Paul explains this good news, when he says that Jesus Christ died for our sins in accordance with the Scriptures.

Sins are whatever we say, do, or think that is contrary to, or negligent of, the expectations of a holy God. His holiness is first defined by right standards that provide a safe and good path for our life and for those whose lives we touch. His holiness is also defined by a right heart that is concerned for justice and love (Rom. 3:26).

When the Apostle Paul says that "Jesus Christ died for our sins," he is summarizing how the standards and the heart of God work together for our good. It is easy for most people to say, "Nobody's perfect," but few naturally consider the impact of that imperfection on our relationship with God. If He is entirely holy, and we sin in thought, word and deed, then our sins separate us from Him. Most people want God

6

to love them, help them with crises and compulsions, and care for their loved ones, but how can we expect God to provide for us, when we have separated ourselves from Him by breaking or neglecting his standards?

The "good news" of the gospel is that God has provided a way for the guilt of our sins to be taken away so that we are not separated from his care now or eternally. God shows his heart by providing for his Son, Jesus Christ, to take the penalty for our sins (1 Pet. 2:24). Because Jesus perfectly kept the standards of God, his holiness fully compensates for our sins. When he died a cruel death on a cross, he bore the punishment for our guilt (1 Pet. 3:18). God's justice and compassion were displayed when he allowed his Son to pay the penalty for our sins – and because Jesus was the Son of God who created the world, his sacrifice was sufficient for the sins of the whole world (1 John 2:2).

What is the proof that Jesus Christ's sacrifice was enough? The Apostle Paul says, "...that he [Jesus] was buried, [and] that he was raised on the third day in accordance with the Scriptures." Jesus' burial proves that he really paid the ultimate price for our sins (he died); and, Jesus' resurrection proves that price was sufficient. God removed the ultimate penalty for our sin, death itself, from Jesus because his suffering and death fully paid for the penalty for our guilt. God's justice and mercy worked together to provide a solution to the sin problem that every imperfect human being has with God. In a "great exchange," Christ took our sin on himself and we received his righteousness (Isaiah 53:6; 2 Cor. 5:21).

2. The Gospel Must Be Received

The good news of the gospel is that God has provided a solution to the sin that separates every person from a Holy God. This provision is a wonderful gift from a good and merciful Heavenly Father. But like all gifts, this one must be received to be enjoyed. —John 1:12–13

We receive the gift of God's forgiveness and eternal love by acknowledging that our sin would separate us from Him if Jesus did not die for our sin. We make this acknowledgement by confessing that we are sinful and need God's help to have the guilt of our sins removed (1 John 1:9). Of course, it does no good to make this confession if we don't believe Jesus really paid the full penalty for our sins. So, our confession needs to be accompanied by faith in Christ's provision.

Faith is not simply the confidence that we have enough faith to make God love and forgive us. That would ultimately be faith in whatever feelings or thoughts that we could muster up inside ourselves—basically trusting that we could generate something strong enough or good enough inside us as the basis of our forgiveness. In essence, such faith would still be trusting in ourselves to provide something to make God love us.

Faith is not trust in what we provide to God; it is total reliance on what God provides for us (Rom. 9:16). Biblical faith receives the gift of Christ's sacrifice as sufficient for paying the full penalty for our sin. Faith is not so much doing as depending—not so much a mental exercise as a spiritual reliance on Jesus' work. We come to God with empty hands and open hearts to receive his gift of love (Eph. 2:8–9). We don't point to our merits or compare ourselves to others' demerits. We don't try to add to God's gift or qualify for it by some extraordinary effort of mind or will. We simply receive God's gift without pretending or protesting that we have to add something to make it good enough. Then, we rest on God's promise to forgive the guilt of all persons who acknowledge that Jesus provided precisely what was needed, and entirely what was needed, to pay the penalty for their sin (Matt. 11:28–30).

When we receive and rest upon Christ alone for our salvation from the earthly guilt and eternal consequences of sin, then the Bible assures us that we will have God's love and help forever. He promises to forgive us and to help us break the patterns of sin that have been a part of our lives. This doesn't immediately make us or our world perfect, but it makes us immensely grateful for the gift of salvation that God has provided.

As a result, we now want to live for the God who loves us so much (John 14:15). Our lives begin to reflect more and more of our love for God, and He provides the Holy Spirit to live inside us and help us honor our Savior and experience his care (2 Cor. 3:18). Spiritual struggles and temptations will still challenge us but, as we respond with love for the God who has been so gracious to us, we grow in our desire and ability to honor Him (Gal. 5:22). We are never again helpless against the compulsions, addictions and patterns of behavior that once seemed to control, or even enslave, us (John 14:26; 1 John 4:4). Our good works do not earn any more of God's love (that only flows through faith in Christ's provision), but rather they show more and more of our love. Always we are responding to grace; never earning it (Eph. 2:10).

God's assurances of the love from Him that we have received by faith alone enables us to face the trials and tragedies of a broken world with confidence that our eternity is secure – and that God is working all things in our lives for our eternal good. So, as we follow him on the good and safe spiritual path described by the standards in his Word, we can know joy and peace even in a world of sadness and pain. Because God's love never fails or diminishes we know that He will never leave or forsake those who are united to Him through faith in Jesus Christ. That is really good news!

3. The Gospel Is Unique

Sometimes people question whether faith in Jesus is

necessary. They may have been affected by the philosophies of this age that commend every religion for having elements of spiritual truth, or as being various paths to the same destination of a relationship with God. At first, such thinking seems very broadminded, but it actually comes from a perspective of pride that keeps people from having to make a commitment to any religion or faith.

The claim that all religions are really the same, demeans the commitments and ideas of those who actually have dedicated themselves to those faith distinctions. The claim comes from those who deliberately stand outside or above all faith distinctions that have been developed and practiced by millions of people across countless centuries and declares that those distinctions are meaningless and their adherents are unenlightened – or, at least, not as informed as the person making the claim of the meaninglessness of faith distinctions. Seen this way, the willingness to dismiss all religious distinctions actually seems like religious bigotry rather than spiritual broadmindedness.

True spiritual integrity respects other religions enough to be honest about their differences (1 Pet. 3:15). Certainly many religions advocate similar moral codes of integrity, morality and generosity, but how those codes are practiced and what they accomplish are significantly different.

The unique feature of Christianity is the claim that such moral codes cannot qualify persons for God's acceptance on earth or in eternity. We and our good deeds will always be flawed and fall short of the holiness of our God ("nobody's perfect"). Therefore, instead of qualifying for a relationship with God by reaching some level of moral goodness or mental transcendence, Christianity teaches that God reaches to us. Because we could not climb to Him, He came to us in the person of Jesus Christ (Phil. 2:5–9). Our hope is not in becoming good enough to come to God, but in trusting that he was good enough to come to us.

Our faith is never in the sufficiency of our good works or thoughts, but in the sufficiency of the gift of Jesus that we receive by faith alone. True love for other persons is not denying this distinction but sharing it with them. We respect other faiths enough to be honest about the unique claims of the Christian gospel, and we love all persons enough to tell them this "good news." We trust that God will deal fairly with all persons in eternity based upon their experiences and deeds on earth (Rom. 1:20), but releasing people from the guilt and fear of trying to measure up to God based upon their accomplishments, rather that faith in his provision is the immediate calling of true compassion (Matt. 28:16–20).

4. The Gospel Is Taught Throughout the Bible

There are many aspects of the gospel beyond our personal salvation. When the Old Testament prophets predicted the coming of the Savior, and when Jesus talked about a kingdom on earth that he would rule as our Lord, the effects were vast: prisoners are set free, slaves unbound, antagonisms quelled, injustices punished, oppression is removed, poverty vanquished, wars cease, and much more "good news" results for our world. All of these elements of our gospel message are the ultimate effects of Christ's Second Coming in power and glory, but they are also the radiating effects of the lives of believers who now live in response to the grace they have received from God (Isa. 42:7; 61:1–6; Jer. 22:3; 30:8).

Mercy and justice inevitably flow from the hearts and convictions of those who have received grace (Mic. 6:8; Luke 15:37; 1 Tim. 6:18; James 2:15–17). The Bible devotes many pages to our mercy and justice concerns, hopes, and obligations. Christ commissions believers with the care of others who are the objects of his affection and we have the obligation of demonstrating his character in every sphere of our careers, communities, and associates (Matt. 25:34–36; Luke 11:49–32; 14:12–14). Still, we need to recognize that the matters of "first importance," as Paul described them were those bearing on salvation from sin (1 Cor. 15:3). Persons will not ultimately benefit if they gain the whole world (i.e., freedom from bonds, poverty, and worry) but lose their souls (Mark 8:36–38). The good news of mercy and equity that radiates from Jesus' heart transforms our world as Christians live the priorities of their Lord.

Our compassion for others and our confidence in the gospel should never be based on personal preferences or cultural traditions. Human authority is an insufficient basis for determining how we can and should relate to God. For this reason, Christians base their understanding of the gospel on the teaching of the Bible that God has inspired for us. From the first page to the last, the Bible is either preparing us for the work of Jesus or detailing its implications for our lives. For this reason, we will need next to consider what the following Chinese scholars say about the Bible and how its many details and dimensions are all leading to this same gospel of salvation from sin by faith in the provision of Jesus Christ.

Bryan Chapell
Stated Clerk of the Presbyterian Church in America
Former President of Covenant Theological Seminary

1

The Gospel Gives Us Union with Christ

James Miao

Since the Protestant Reformation, justification by faith alone has often been regarded as the core doctrine of Christianity. Martin Luther discovered justification by faith alone in the Book of Romans and consequently led the church out of the error of justification on the basis of merit and works. Theologians also generally define the core of Paul's theology as "justification by faith alone," and they say that this is the main theme of both the Book of Romans and the Book of Galatians.

This view often causes people to focus on justification over sanctification in their analysis of the gospel. We often even equate justification with salvation itself. We are thankful that God has freely justified us in Christ, and we assume that this constitutes the whole of salvation. We consider sanctification to be based on justification — justification is the "gospel" while sanctification seems to be something other than the gospel, a mere response to justification. It is the "Christian life" or "spiritual discipline." This way of thinking ignores the fact that God has sanctified us in Christ. Christ is both our righteousness and our holiness. The good news of Christ's death and resurrection not only brings us the grace of justification but also the grace of sanctification. A gospel without sanctification, therefore, is not a complete gospel.

Being Justified and Sanctified Simultaneously

Some theologians have proposed the concept of the ordo salutis ("order of salvation"). For example, John Murray suggests the following order in which God executes salvation: calling, regeneration, faith, repentance, adoption, sanctification, perseverance, glorification. He believes that justification is a momentary act while sanctification is a consequent process.[1] But theologians such as Louis Berkhof believe that this order is only a logical order and not a chronological order. Anthony Hoekema believes that the salvation with which God provides us in Jesus Christ is too rich. Words such as justification and sancfication simply describe different aspects of the spiritual blessings we receive in salvation. Justification describes God's forgiveness of our sins from the perspective of the law— Jesus's righteousness is credited to us, and we are declared righteous. Sanctification, on the other hand, refers to our moral and spiritual renewal.[2]

Justification and sanctification are both graces that God freely gives us in Jesus Christ, and they are simulneously obtained when we repent and believe in the Lord. Paul says, "You were washed, you were sanctified, you were justified in the name of the Lord Jesus Christ and by the Spirit of our God" (1 Cor. 6:11b). In the original, the words "sanctified" and "justified" are in the past tense, and "sanctified" is listed before "justified." This indicates that sanctification and jutification are both blessings that we obtain the moment we believe in the Lord. Archibald Robertson believes that we obtain both blessings before we are baptized.[3]

The fall of Adam brought about a twofold calamity on mankind: first, man must face punishment for his sin; second, because his nature is entirely corrupt, he cannot save himself from sin. The grace that God gives us in the gospel addresses every aspect of our brokenness. Justification solves the first problem above. Jesus Christ substitutes himself for us on the cross, the righteous for the unrighteous. He bears the punishment for our sins and becomes our righteousness. Sanctification, on the other hand, solves the second problem. Through his death, Jesus brings our body of sin to nothing, and, through his resurrection, he gives us a new, holy life.

The essence of salvation is union with Jesus Christ. That is to say, through faith, through the power of the Holy Spirit, we are able to enter into a personal, deep, real union with the incarnate, crucified, risen Savior Jesus Christ. This comes about by means of our receiving every spiritual blessing (Eph. 1:3). Our union with Christ by faith brings us not only the blessing of justification but also the blessing of sanctification. Paul says, "And because of him you are in Christ Jesus, who became to us wisdom from God, righteousness and sanctification and redemption" (1 Cor. 1:30). Sanctification is one of the blessings listed here that Christ brings us. Justification and sanctification are not accomplished by human effort. Jesus accomplishes them for us. We only need to receive them by faith. The gospel not only justifies us by faith but sanctifies us by faith.

John Calvin's soteriology in his *Institutes of the Christian Religion* begins with union with Christ.[4] Calvin says that righteousness and sanctification are inseparable just like the sun's rays and heat are inseparable. "The sun by its heat quickens and fertilises the earth; by its rays enlightens and illumines it. Here is a mutual and undivided connection, and yet reason itself prohibits us from transferring the peculiar properties of the one to the other."[5] When we are united with Christ, we immediately receive two blessings: justification and sanctification. And these two blessings are inseparable. One is always accompanied by the other. Separating justification from sanctification is tantamount to dismembering Christ. In the minds of many believers, jutification is the first step to salvation, and sanctification is the second step. Justification is viewed as free grace that is obtained by faith, while sanctification is obtained only after much effort. They think that all Christians are justified but not necessarily sanctified—sanctification is only for those few mature Christians. In reality, though, all Christians are justified and sanctified. Sanctification is not a benefit apart from justification that is obtained by works. The two are inseparable.

Jesus Is Our Sanctification

And because of him you are in Christ Jesus, who became to us wisdom from God, righteousness and satification and redemption. —1 Corinthians 1:30

Paul here claims that Jesus became to us sanctification. He does not mean that Jesus sanctifies us. He means that Jesus himself is our sanctification.

We polluted and unclean people are totally depraved. How, then, does Jesus become our sanctification? Jesus says, "For their sake I consecrate myself, that they also may be sanctified in truth" (John 17:19). Thomas F. Torrance calls this Christ's "self-sanctification" as Incarnate Son.[6]

From the moment he was conceived by the Holy Spirit, Jesus consecrated his own humanity in Mary's womb (Luke 1:35). He lived a completely holy life in a world full of sin and temptation. He continually grew in wisdom and stature and obedience to the will of God. He did not go from being imperfect to perfect but from being a baby to an adult. When he shouted "It is finished!" on the cross (John 19:30), he gave himself up to his Father. He was the first man to be sanctified through his own obedience. When he rose from the dead and ascended, his glorified humanity contained an indestructible life (Heb. 7:16).When God sanctifies us in Christ, he is actually performing a work of recreation. In the beginning, God created us in his image (Gen 1:27). But we have become depraved in Adam's sin (Rom. 5:12–21), and this image has been distorted. From the very beginning of the Old Testament and throughout all of human history, we see the terrible consequences of all of this. Jesus came to us in the flesh and showed us once again the glorious image of God (John 1:14). "He is the image of the invisible God" (Col. 1:15a). "He is the radiance of the glory of God and the exact imprint of his nature" (Heb. 1:3a). God wants to recreate us through Jesus Christ so that we might possess the glorious image of God once again. "For those whom he foreknew he also predestined to be conformed to the image of his Son, in order that he might be the firstborn among many brothers" (Rom. 8:29).

Jesus is the perfect man and the perfect image of God. The essence and goal of sanctification is to reflect the image of Jesus Christ,[7] and we do not obtain this through our own moral efforts but through union with Christ.

Being United to Jesus In His Death and Resurrection

[Jesus] was delivered up for our trespasses and raised for our justification. —Romans 4:25

We often only discuss the importance of Christ's death and resurrection as they relate to justification, but they should also serve as a paradigm for understanding sanctification. Just as justification includes negative aspects—through Christ's death we are not condemned—as well as positive aspects—through Christ's resurrection we are justified (Rom. 4:25), sanctification also includes negative aspects—through Christ's death our sinful nature is crucified (Rom. 6:6; Gal. 2:20; Col. 3:3–5) as well as positive aspects—through Christ's resurrection we live new lives (Rom. 6:4, 11; Col. 3:1; Phil. 3:10).

As we all know, we are justified by participating in Christ's death and resurrection. When we are united with him in his death and burial, our sins are forgiven and we are freed from condemnation. And when we are united with him in his resurrection, we are declared righteous. But the benefits we obtain by being united with Christ in his death and resurrection should also extend to our sanctification. We are also sanctified by participating in Christ's death and resurrection. God mysteriously unites us to Christ. His death and resurrection should not merely be regarded as personal events that he experienced but as redemptive facts—in him we are crucified with him, buried with him, and risen with him (Gal. 2:20; Eph. 2:6; Heb. 2:12). Through this redemptive fact, the power of sin has been vanquished and we have received new life. In other words, this event has a real effect in the lives of those who are united to him.

Paul discusses this in detail in Romans 6. He imagines someone talking to him who believes that someone who lives in grace can continue to sin so that God's grace may abound (Rom. 6:1–2). Paul categorically denies this. He says, "Do you not know that all of us who have been baptized into Christ Jesus were baptized into his death? We were buried therefore with him by baptism into death, in order that, just as Christ was raised from the dead by the glory of the Father, we too might walk in newness of life" (Rom. 6:3–4). Paul doesn't say, "Do you not know that all of us should act with gratitude for God's freely justifying us in Christ?" Paul roots his answer in the redemptive effect of our being united with Christ: We have actually participated in Christ's death, burial, and resurrection, and this sanctifies us. The questioner obviously does not understand the meaning of union with Christ.

Paul's answer is primarily based on two main points. The first is that we are united with Christ in his death. "We know that our old self was crucified with him in order that the body of sin might be brought to nothing, so that we would no longer be enslaved to sin" (Rom. 6:6). The second is that we are united with Christ in his resurrection, which causes to walk in newness of life (Rom. 6:4). Our particiption in the death of Christ frees us from the bondage of sin, and our participation in his resurrection enables us to live to God in righteousness. What Paul is saying here is that as long as we apply to ourselves the blessing of being united to Christ, we can live a holy life.

Definitive Sanctification and Progressive Sanctification

Those who have been united with Christ have become new men. But the likeness of our old self is still present in our lives. As Paul writes in Romans 7: "For I delight in the law of God, in my inner being, but I see in my members another law waging war against the law of my mind and making me captive to the law of sin that dwells in my members. Wretched man that I am! Who will deliver me from this body of death?" (Rom. 7:22–24). Paul feels as though two people are simultaneously living inside of him—his pre-conversion self and his post-conversion self. These two selves are evenly matched and are fighting against each other. Many times, it seems as though our old self has the upper hand. Sometimes we even feel like we have split personalities. Watchman Nee describes this battle as one between spirit and soul.[8] The Christian's spirit has been saved, but his soul has yet to be saved. The soul must be broken before the spirit can come out.

When we look at how sanctification is described in the Bible, we find that there are two aspects to it: it is both a definitive, once-for-all fact and a progressive, continuous, life-long process. In order to properly understand the battles in our lives, we must understand both the definitive and progressive natures of sanctification. For our union with Christ is both definitive—we are inextricably united with him forever—and at the same time progressive. Therefore, we continually grow in our union with him until we become mature and attain to the whole measure of the fullness of Christ. If we want to understand sanctication correctly, we must pay attention to both aspects.

1. Definitive Sanctification

In the New Testament, sanctification is most commonly described not in progressive terms but in once-for-all, decisive terms. As mentioned above, Paul often asserts that believers are already sanctified in their present condition (1 Cor. 1:2, 6:11). Even though sin still lingers in the lives of believers, they are nevertheless called "saints" in Christ (Phil. 1:1; Col. 1:2; 1 Cor. 1:2).

Many people think that a believer can only achieve a sanctified state in eternity or only after attaining a relatively good spiritual state—even sinlessness—through hard work. But the Bible says that every Christian is a saint. Moreover, when it says that Christians are sanctified, it usually uses the passive voice and the perfect tense (Acts 20:32, 26:18). The Bible tells us it is a fact that every Christian has been united to Jesus Christ. In this union, we are mysteriously yet truly crucified, buried, and resurrected (1 Cor. 1:30; Rom. 6:3–5; Col. 2:12, 3:1). Through this union, our sinful nature has been killed, and we have been resurrected with Christ. "Even when we were dead in our trespasses, [God] made us alive together with Christ—by grace you have been saved—and raised us up with him and seated us with him in the heavenly places in Christ Jesus" (Eph. 2:5–6).

In order to sanctify us, God kills our sinful nature through the death of Christ and gives us new life through his resurrection. Our sanctification in Christ is definitive. Since we have been united to Christ, we have been sanctified in him. Our holiness is bound to him. Because he is a holy man, we are also holy men (saints) in him. We will never lose our sanctified state, just as we will never lose our justified state. "But you were washed, you were sanctified, you were justified in the name of the Lord Jesus Christ and by the Spirit of our God" (1 Cor. 6:11b).

What does it mean that we have been definitively sanctified in Christ?

This means that through our participation in the death of Christ, the power of sin over us has been decisively broken; and, through participation in the resurrection of Christ, we also truly and definitely experience new life. "So you also must consider yourselves dead to sin and alive to

God in Christ Jesus" (Rom. 6:11). "Therefore, if anyone is in Christ, he is a new creation. The old has passed away; behold, the new has come" (2 Cor. 5:17).

This means that those in Christ truly have a new life. They have experienced a renewed life through dying and rising with Christ. But this does not mean that Christians have entered a perfect state of sinlessness where they no longer struggle with sin. If we declare that we have no sin, we only increase it (1 John 1:8). Although sin still exists in us, its power has been decisively broken. It has now lost its citizenship and became an illegal immigrant, although it will take time to fully deport it.

2. Progressive Sanctification

Progressive sanctification means that believers prgressively and continuously experience the benefits of sanctification in Christ. God will continue to complete the work that he has already begun in us, transforming us more and more into the image of his son (Phil. 1:6; Rom. 8:29). "We are to grow up in every way into him who is the head, into Christ" (Eph. 4:15). Most importantly, we are continually transformed into the image of Jesus Christ through fighting against the remaining sin in our lives. This is a day-by-day, year-by-year process that lasts our whole life. Through this process, God will fulfill his promise to us in Christ Jesus—he will not leave us in sin but will accomplish the work he has begun (Phil. 1:6).

We have been definitively united to Christ and consequently justified, sanctified, and adopted. On this basis, our relationship with him is growing day by day. We experience in deeper ways the peace that forgiveness brings. We grow in holiness and become more and more like his children. He is for us the source of grace, the bread of life, and the water of life. From him we obtain endless blessings. "And we all, with unveiled face, beholding the glory of the Lord, are being transformed into the same image from one degree of glory to another. For this comes from the Lord who is the Spirit" (2 Cor. 3:18).

The Work of the Holy Spirit

There is no doubt that the role of the Holy Spirit in sanctification is crucial, but we need to clarify some things. We often emphasize the work of Christ in the doctrines of atonement and justification, while we emphasize the work of the Holy Spirit in the doctrine of sanctification. We must realize that the Holy Spirit does not replace Jesus in doing the work of sanctification so that Jesus is absent in our sanctification. The primary purpose of the Holy Spirit in sanctification is to convey to us the presence and power of Christ, who is our holiness. The Holy Spirit is essential to our holiness. Because his indwelling presence convinces us that the holy Christ is with us, we can die to sin and live to God. Our union with Christ occurs through the power and indwelling of the Spirit, who unites us to Christ. The indwelling Spirit is the "spirit of Christ" (Gal. 4:6; Phil. 1:19).

Paul elaborates on this in Romans: "You, however, are not in the flesh but in the Spirit, if in fact the Spirit of God dwells in you. Anyone who does not have the Spirit of Christ does not belong to him. But if Christ is in you, although the body is dead because of sin, the Spirit is life because of righteousness. If the Spirit of him who raised Jesus from the dead dwells in you, he who raised Christ Jesus from the dead will also give life to your mortal bodies through his Spirit who dwells in you" (Rom. 8:9–11).

John Murray discusses the relationship between the Holy Spirit and Jesus Christ in our sanctification in this way: "It is as the Spirit of Christ and as the Spirit of him who raised up Christ from the dead that the Holy Spirit sanctifies."[9] We must not think that the Holy Spirit works in us apart from the resurrected and glorified Christ. Satification depends on the death and resurrection of Christ, not only in the beginning but throughout the whole process. The process of sanctification is a process in which the Holy Spirit continually applies Jesus's resurrection to us.

Sanctification Cannot Be Achieved through Moralism

Sanctification is a work that God does in Christ through the Holy Spirit. Man cannot be sanctified by relying on his own efforts because holiness is not merely a change in external behavior. It is first and foremost a renewal of one's nature, which comes by being united to Christ in his death and resurrection. The death of Christ has brought the body of sin to nothing, and his resurrection has given us new life. What we need is for these things to be applied to us through faith.

Over the past few years, we have repeatedly emphasized that we must not live according to religion but according to the gospel. Religion says, "I obey; therefore, God accepts me." The gospel says, "God accepts me through Christ; therefore, I obey." This changes our motive for pursuing holiness. We no longer live as we once did under the bondage of religion in which we attempt to become justified by relying on sanctification. To some extent, this can bring us rest and comfort. But "gospel-drivenness" only solves the problem of pursuing sanctification at the level of motivation. In essence, we still must rely on ourselves to achieve sanctification because our gospel still only concerns justification. Sanctification is understood as a response to salvation rather than the content of salvation. In reality, sanctification and justification are both aspects of salvation. We often think that pursuing sanctification means being grateful for being freely justified, but in reality we should also be grateful for sanctification.

Many people think that chapters 1-11 in Romans discuss justification, while chapter 12 discusses sanctification. In reality, Paul does not only discuss justification in chapters 1-11. He also discusses sanctification (chapters 6-8). The gospel includes not only justification but also sanctification. Sanctification is also a grace given to us in the gospel. It is not the result of our own efforts.

Sanctification by Faith Alone

The gospel is not a set of ethical directives. It is something that God has already done for us. Jesus has become our wisdom, righteousness, sanctification, and redemption. We need only to receive these things by faith, then they are ours. The first thing we need in order to pursue sanctification is faith. We are not only justified by faith but also sanctified by faith. If we only know justification by faith alone, then we only believe half of the gospel.

This is what Paul teaches in Romans: "So you also must consider yourselves dead to sin and alive to God in Christ Jesus. Let not sin therefore reign in your mortal body, to make you obey its passions. Do not present your members to sin as instruments for unrighteousness, but present yourselves to God as those who have been brought from death to life, and your members to God as instruments for righteousness" (Rom. 6:11–13). The word "consider" in this passage is very important because it tells us that our pursuit of sanctification must first be based on faith in our union with Christ in his death and resurrection. We must believe that we have already died to sin in Christ and live to

God. A similar argument appears in Colossians 3 where we read that we must "seek the things that are above" and "put to death what is earthly in us" because we have already died and been resurrected in Christ (verses 1-5).

In short, when we say that we belong to Christ, we have actually died to sin through his death and risen from the dead through his resurrection. The fact that we have participated in the death and resurrection of Christ is the basis of our sanctification (Gal. 2:20). Paul does teach or urge believers to pursue sanctification in a moralistic way. His admonitions are rooted in his belief that believers have died with Christ and risen with him. He does not say, "You should live a holy life because Christ has died and risen for you." He says, "You should live a holy life because you have already died and risen with Christ."

Faith is not a tool that merely enables us to embrace Christ in the first place. It also enables us to continually receive his sanctifying work in us. As Calvin says, "[Christ] not only unites us to himself by an undivided bond of fellowship, but by a wondrous communion brings us daily into closer connection, until he becomes altogether one with us."[10] As we grow in faith, we increasingly transform into the image of Christ (Col. 2:6–7; Eph. 4:11-13). The root of sin lies in our unbelief. We do not believe what Christ has done for us. We still want to sanctify ourselves. Satan also continually tempts us to repeat the same sins and tries to make us doubt what Christ has done for us, causing us to fall again into the trap of self-sanctification. So sanctification is largely about strengthening our faith so that we might be confident in the gospel and live out what we believe. This is why we must continually preach the gospel in church. We are not only justified by faith alone but sanctified by faith alone.

The Seriousness of Christian Sin

We should believe the fact that we have been sanctified in Christ. We are new men. God has recreated us and is still recreating us.

James Sawyer says, "We do not see ourselves merely within the limited vision of our own biographies: Volume One, the life of slavery to sin; Volume Two, the life of freedom from sin. We see ourselves set in a cosmic context: in Adam by nature, in Christ by grace."[11] From this perspective, sin is contradictory to the Christian life. If we sin, we not only violate the law, we also deny the fact that we are in Christ. Sin is a kind of "decreation." This is why we must deal seriously with sin in the church.

Paul and John do not treat Christian sin lightly like mere moral failures. They believe that sin conflicts with our very existence. Believers have truly been united to Jesus Christ and have new life in him. We have been recreated in the image of Jesus Christ. The presence of sin in a believer is terrible and inconceivable because it subverts reality.

Do you not know that your bodies are members of

Christ? Shall I then take the members of Christ and make them members of a prostitute? Never!—1 Corinthians 6:15

Or do you not know that your body is a temple of the Holy Spirit within you, whom you have from God? You are not your own.—1 Corinthians 6:15

Do you not know that all of us who have been baptized into Christ Jesus were baptized into his death?—Romans 6:3

No one who abides in him keeps on sinning. —1 John 3:6a

Christian sin is a terrible self-contradiction. It is not only a moral problem—most importantly, it is a lack of belief in the gospel.

The Word of God

How do we maintain and strengthen our faith?

First, we do so through the Word of God. "So faith comes from hearing, and hearing through the word of Christ" (Rom. 10:17). Calvin says, "The true knowledge of Christ consists in receiving him as he is offered by the Father— namely, as invested with his gospel. For, as he is appointed as the end of our faith, so we cannot directly tend towards him except under the guidance of the gospel."[12]   Jesus prays to the Father, "Sanctify them in the truth; your word is truth" (John 17:17). We accept Christ through his Word and continue to live in him through his Word. "Therefore, as you received Christ Jesus the Lord, so walk in him, rooted and built up in him and established in the faith, just as you were taught, abounding in thanksgiving" (Col. 2:6–7). "All Scripture is breathed out by God and profitable for teaching, for reproof, for correction, and for training in righteousness, that the man of God may be complete, equipped for every good work" (2 Tim. 3:16–17).

We must preach the Word of God in public worship, but we must not preach legalistic sermons. We must preach the gospel. We must preach Christ-centered sermons. We must proclaim the good news of Christ's death and resurrection for us. In our daily, personal devotions, we must meet Christ invested with his gospel.

The Sacraments

The sacraments are the Word made visible and are intended to strengthen our faith.

The sacraments include baptism and communion. Baptism is a sign that we have been incorporated into Christ's death and resurrection. The sacrament of communion is the Lord's Supper, by which we continue to receive the crucified and risen Christ and to be nourished by him. When we share the bread and the cup, we are sharing Christ. "The cup of blessing that we bless, is it not a participation in the blood of Christ? The bread that we break, is it not a participation in the body of Christ?" (1 Cor. 10:16). Christ is so truly present that to not recognize the reality of his presence is to profane his body and blood (1 Cor. 11:27–29). Just as we accept Christ through the preached Word, we continue to grow in union with Christ through the visible Word.

Therefore, the sacraments function in the same way as the Word of God. They present Christ to us, in whom are hidden all the riches of grace.

A Community of Shared Life

When believers are united to Christ, they are also smultaneously united to other members (1 Cor. 12:12, 27). Therefore, our holiness is contained in the holiness of the body of Christ and in the holiness of other members. Sanctification only happens when we are united to Christ, but union with Christ is a matter for the whole body.

Sanctification is not a personal matter because our personal holiness (or lack of holiness) is influenced by and influences the holiness of the whole body (1 Cor. 5:6, 8:12). If our own union with Christ is a very real and personal union, then so is our union with each other.

We grow together in holiness. "Rather, speaking the truth in love, we are to grow up in every way into him who is the head, into Christ, from whom the whole body, joined and held together by every joint with which it is equipped, when each part is working properly, makes the body grow so that it builds itself up in love" (Eph. 4:15–16).

Suffering

Christians are people who have been united to Christ. When Christ was on earth, he carried a cross to Calvary. The Christian life is likewise the way of the cross. To be united with Christ is to live as a member of his body, which will necessarily involve suffering with him. Christ's life was marked by suffering, humiliation, rejection, and a cross. Therefore, when Christians encounter trials in their lives, they should not be surprised (in fact, they can find comfort in them).

"Beloved, do not be surprised at the fiery trial when it comes upon you to test you, as though something strange were happening to you. But rejoice insofar as you share Christ's sufferings" (1 Pet. 4:12–13a). Paul points out that to suffer is to share in the suffering and death of Christ. His sufferings and tribulations are proofs and manifestations of the fact that Christ is in him. "[We are] always carrying in the body the death of Jesus, so that the life of Jesus may also be manifested in our bodies. For we who live are always being given over to death for Jesus's sake, so that the life of Jesus also may be manifested in our mortal flesh" (2 Cor. 4:10–11). "...that I may know him and the power of his resurrection, and may share his sufferings, becoming like him in his death, that by any means possible

I may attain the resurrection from the dead" (Phil. 3:10–11). Suffering, persecution, trials, and rejection are the hallmarks of the Christian life because they manifest Christ's own life. As Martin Luther wrote, "The holy Christian people are externally recognized by the holy possession of the sacred cross. They must endure every misfortune and persecution, all kinds of trials and evil from the devil, the world, and the flesh...by inward sadness, timidity, fear, outward poverty, contempt, illness, and weakness, in order to become like their head, Christ."[13]

The world may praise our moral behavior, but when, through sanctification, we become more like Christ, they may mock us. "If the world hates you, know that it has hated me before it hated you. If you were of the world, the world would love you as its own; but because you are not of the world, but I chose you out of the world, therefore the world hates you" (John 15:18–19). The world was offended by Christ's life and death because he perfectly reflected the holy image of God, and this image is an indictment against fallen humanity. Just as God revealed himself through the suffering, persecution, humiliation, and death of Christ, we can expect that God will continue to reveal himself through the body of Christ—the church—in the same way.

Conclusion

The gospel is good news. It is a great thing that Jesus

Christ has accomplished for us. He died and rose from the dead for us, giving us every spiritual blessing. We do not need to earn these blessings through our own merit. We only need to obtain them by faith. By faith we are united with him in his death and resurrection. We are justified by faith alone, and we are sanctified by faith alone.

Through the death of Christ, our corrupt and fallen natures have been put to death, and through his resurrection, we have new life. Through his Spirit, God unites us with Jesus Christ, who was sanctified for us, and incorporates us into his death and resurrection, which conquers sin and gives us life.

We have been sanctified, and we are also being sanctified—we increasingly bear the image of Jesus Christ. God calls us to participate in this creative work to restore his image.

James Miao holds a Master of Divinity and has served as a house church pastor for over 20 years. He is a lecturer in seminary and is a father of three children.

Further Reflection:

• How does Miao keep Christ central in his definition and application of the doctrine of sanctification?

• What are the dangers of focusing on justification and ignoring union with Christ in our theology? How might Western culture's focus on the individual vs. Asian culture's focus on the collective influence our ideas of justification and sanctification?

• Miao suggests four means of sanctification: Scripture, the sacraments, a shared life with other believers, and suffering. Which of these do you struggle with in your walk with Christ? What steps could you take to experience union with Christ in each of these areas?

2

The Gospel Restores Intimacy with God

James Qin

That which was from the beginning, which we have heard, which we have seen with our eyes, which we looked upon and have touched with our hands, concerning the word of life—the life was made manifest, and we have seen it, and testify to it and proclaim to you the eternal life, which was with the Father and was made manifest to us—that which we have seen and heard we proclaim also to you, so that you too may have fellowship with us; and indeed our fellowship is with the Father and with his Son Jesus Christ. And we are writing these things so that our joy may be complete. —1 John 1:1-4

The Greek word *koinonia* is translated into Chinese as "fellowship." It basically means "interaction," "intimacy," or "sharing." Here we can simply understand "fellowship" as an intimate relationship formed by two (or more) people through sharing something together.

Fellowship in the Bible includes fellowship within the

Trinity, fellowship between God and man, and fellowship between man and man.

The apostle John talks about three types of fellowship: fellowship between the Son ("the word of life") and the Father, fellowship between the apostles, the Father, and his Son Jesus Christ, and fellowship between the saints ("you…have fellowship with us").

In this article, I will begin by discussing fellowship within the Trinity and then move on to discuss the gospel story of God's fellowship with man as revealed through redemptive history—how God reveals his fellowship with man through creation, judgment, redemption, and renewal. Finally, I will consider how Christians can live lives of love, gratitude, passion, and joy by practicing fellowship with God.

Fellowship Within the Trinity

What Is God Like?

Some people think that God is a kind of impersonal energy force that was the first cause of the universe. Others think that God is the supreme Lord of the universe. Some of these views are wrong, and others are incomplete. The Bible reveals that God is a personal God and a triune God. "God eternally exists as three persons, Father, Son, and Holy Spirit, and each person is fully God, and there is one God."[14]   Although it is quite difficult to accurately understand and express the concept of the Trinity, this is a very important truth in Scripture.

You may ask, "What was God doing in eternity before

he created heaven and earth? Was he lonely?" We must admit that as creatures, our knowledge of God is extremely limited. We can only know certain truths that God has revealed about himself by reverently and humbly studying Scripture. The Gospel of John records a passionate prayer of Jesus to his Father. It includes the following words: "Father, I desire that they also, whom you have given me, may be with me where I am, to see my glory that you have given me because you loved me before the foundation of the world" (John 17:24). This verse reveals that before the creation of all things, before anything else happened, the Father loved his Son in eternity.

In his book *Delighting in the Trinity*, Michael Reeves says, "So it is not just that the Father loves the Son; the Son also loves the Father—and so much so that to do his Father's pleasure is as food to him...It is his sheer joy and delight always to do as his Father says."[15] "But I do as the Father has commanded me, so that the world may know that I love the Father" (John 14:31).

"And it is through the Spirit that the Father declares his love for the Son."[16] "And the Holy Spirit descended on him in bodily form, like a dove; and a voice came from heaven, 'You are my beloved Son; with you I am well pleased'" (Luke 3:22).

"It is all deeply personal: the Spirit stirs up the delight of the Father in the Son and the delight of the Son in the Father, inflaming their love and so binding them together in 'the fellowship of the Holy Spirit.'"[17]

Therefore, before creation, the triune God was neither

alone nor bored, but the three persons in eternity deeply loved each other and were satisfied in each other. The three persons of the Trinity share the same divinity and essence. They share a relationship of unity and fellowship. The Father and the Son are relations—the Father exists in relation to the Son, and the Son exists in relation to the Father. The triune nature of the Godhead ensures that the three persons can experience complete love for and satisfaction in each other. "Richard [of Saint Victor] argued that if God were just one person, he could not be intrinsically loving, since for all eternity (before creation) he would have had nobody to love. If there were two persons, he went on, God might be loving, but in an excluding, ungenerous way. After all, when two persons love each other, they can be so infatuated with each other that they simply ignore everyone else—and a God like that would be very far from good news. But when the love between two persons is happy, healthy and secure, they rejoice to share it. Just so it is with God, said Richard. Being perfectly loving, from all eternity the Father and the Son have delighted to share their love and joy with and through the Spirit."[18]

Fellowship Between God and Man

God Establishes Fellowship with Man through Creation.

The first sentence in the Bible declares that in the beginning, God created heaven and earth and all things. But if the members of the Godhead were already experiencing eternal and mutual fellowship and satisfaction, why did God perform this work of creation? It was obviously not because God needed to create some people and things to entertain himself because he was lonely or bored. Rather, creation was an extension of the mutual love and satisfaction within the triune God. The abundant, mutual love between the members of the Godhead overflowed in a creative act. The role of a father is to give life to and to raise children. As eternal Father, "God is an inherently outgoing, lifegiving God."[19] The Father is like an inexhaustible spring that eternally pours forth life and love. The Son is he whom the Father eternally loves. Creation is an extension of this mutual love within the Godhead (an extension of God's love, not God himself), that creation might also enjoy the love of the triune God. The Bible says, "The God who made the world and everything in it, being Lord of heaven and earth, does not live in temples made by man, nor is he served by human hands, as though he needed anything, since he himself gives to all mankind life and breath and everything" (Acts 17:24–25).

The climax of God's creative work was his creation of man. Man was created in the image and likeness of God. Therefore, man is similar to God. God shares his communicable attributes with man. For example, God is love; therefore, man shares with God a limited capacity to love. As the image of God with a body and a soul, man can have true and direct fellowship with God. He could see the face of God in the garden of Eden. He could walk with God and talk with God. He submitted to God's authority and had a wonderful relationship with him. Of all created things, man was the most loved and blessed by God. God made him his representative to rule on earth.

God Breaks Fellowship with Man in Judgment

God entered into harmonious fellowship with man on the condition that man would submit to his authority. However, Adam quickly succumbed to the Devil's temptations and violated God's prohibition. From then on, Adam's relationship with God was broken. So God withdrew his love and grace from Adam and in wrath justly judged him. Adam was driven by God out of the garden of Eden and away from the face of God. The fellowship between God and Adam was broken.

As a representative of mankind, Adam's rebellion plunged all mankind into rebellion against and alienation from God (Rom. 5:12). This was the darkest moment for all mankind. Since then, man no longer knows or worships God. Instead, he worships idols and false gods, which incites even more wrath from God. "For the wrath of God is revealed from heaven against all ungodliness and unriteouness of men, who by their unrighteousness suppress the truth... For although they knew God, they did not honor him as God or give thanks to him, but they became futile in their thinking, and their foolish hearts were darkened. Claiming to be wise, they became fools, and exchanged the glory of the immortal God for images resembling mortal man and birds and animals and creeping things" (Rom. 1:18, 21–23).

God Restores Fellowship with Man through
Redemption

After God broke fellowship with humanity, on the one hand he continued to judge humanity in righteousness. But on the other hand, in love he actively prepared to redeem mankind so that he might restore fellowship with them. All of redemptive history is the history of God restoring fellowship with man. Beginning with the first descendant of Adam, we see God accepting Abel's sacrifice (Gen. 4:4); we see him hearing Seth's prayer (Gen. 4:26); we see Enoch walking with God for three hundred years (Gen. 5:22, 24); we see God walking with Noah in the midst of a wicked generation (Gen. 6:9); we see God blessing Abraham and calling him a friend (James 2:23); we see God communing with Moses on the holy mountain for ten days and showing him his glory (Exod. 4); we see David experiencing intimate fellowship with God many times (Ps. 16, 344, 40, 63).[20] Even though God had active fellowship with his elect in the Old Testament, the group he had fellowship with was limited to the Israelites, and it was as though this fellowship between God and man was separated by a veil.

But in these last days, God has directly sent his only Son into the world. The Son of God came into the world in the flesh and experienced fellowship with man face-to-face. "And the Word became flesh and dwelt among us, and we have seen his glory, glory as of the only Son from the Father, full of grace and truth" (John 1:14).

As fully God and fully man, Jesus Christ had fellowship

with man. That is to say, God had fellowship with man. The incarnation allowed man to experience fellowship with God directly—to hear him, to see him, to touch him. "That which was from the beginning, which we have heard, which we have seen with our eyes, which we looked upon and have touched with our hands, concerning the word of life" (1 John 1:1).

Through Jesus's obedience, death, and resurrection, Jesus accomplished his mediatorial work, restoring man's relationship with God. "All this is from God, who through Christ reconciled us to himself and gave us the ministry of reconciliation" (2 Cor. 5:18). In Christ, God's fellowship with man reached an unprecedented level.

Now, Jesus Christ has ascended to the right hand of God the Father and has sent a Helper—the Holy Spirit—to be with believers forever (John 14:16). Through the indwelling of the Holy Spirit, the believer is brought back into vibrant fellowship with the triune God. The fellowship between the Holy Spirit and the believer is fellowship between the Son and the believer and is also fellowship between the Father and the believer. "And I will ask the Father, and he will give you another Helper, to be with you forever, even the Spirit of truth, whom the world cannot receive, because it neither sees him nor knows him. You know him, for he dwells with you and will be in you...In that day you will know that I am in my Father, and you in me, and I in you" (John 14:16–17, 20).

In Christ, believers have been brought back into fellowship with God, but because the kingdom of God has not yet fully arrived, saints will still experience weaknesses and fall into sins in this life, which will hinder our fellowship with God or occasionally cause us to fall out of fellowship with him. But our fellowship with him will not be broken completely or forever. Nothing can separate us from the love of God. "For I am sure that neither death nor life, nor angels nor rulers, nor things present nor things to come, nor powers, nor height nor depth, nor anything else in all creation, will be able to separate us from the love of God in Christ Jesus our Lord" (Rom. 8:38–39).

God's Fellowship with Man Is Perfected in the New Heaven and New Earth

When Jesus Christ returns, we will see him "face to face" (1 Cor. 13:12). At that time, our fellowship with God will be perfected and will last forever. God will never again hide his face from us, for in the new heaven and new earth, sin and death will be no more. At that time, we will live and reign with God forever and ever. "And I heard a loud voice from the throne saying, 'Behold, the dwelling place of God is with man. He will dwell with them, and they will be his people, and God himself will be with them as their God'" (Rev. 21:3). "No longer will there be anything accursed, but the throne of God and of the Lamb will be in it, and his servants will worship him. They will see his face, and his name will be on their foreheads. And night will be no more. They will need no light of lamp or sun, for the Lord God will be their light, and they will reign forever and ever" (Rev. 22:3–5).

Practicing Fellowship with God

When God, of his own initiative, seeks fellowship with man, man must also actively respond. When man experiences genuine fellowship with God, he will live a life of love, passion, and joy.

Fellowship with God, Not a Business Transaction

On the whole, Chinese culture focuses on relationships, but the kind of relationships that we normally focus on are those that are profitable to us. We do not understand simple relationships that do not involve "benefits." We do not believe in love without an ulterior motive. This way of thinking also affects our understanding of religion. We are deeply inclined to think of religion as a kind of business transaction.

My cousin has an eight-year-old son. After listening to me tell a Bible story about the second coming of Christ, this little boy once blurted out, "So after we survive the final judgment, we don't need to believe in Jesus anymore." This way of thinking is the typical transactional model of religion: I worship some god according to a set of fixed requirements and then ask him to give me various blessings and help me through various difficulties. After all is said and done, everyone waves goodbye. We do not owe anything to each other. We have no obligations to each other. We do not bother each other. People only love the blessings of the gods; they do not love the gods themselves. If you made someone to live with these gods now or in the future, he would be very reluctant or even consider it a curse.

Transactional religion does not care about what the god in whom you believe is like. What is important is whether this god is effective, whether he can provide me with practical benefits. As long as he can provide me with benefits, I will worship him, regardless of which god he is.

Our belief in the triune God, however, is not a business transaction but a relationship. Even though God does bless us, behind this blessing is God's deep love for us. It is his love that overcomes us and draws us to him. "The LORD appeared to us in the past, saying: 'I have loved you with an everlasting love; I have drawn you with unfailing kindness'" (Jer. 31:3). We should respond with gratitude to God's love from the depths of our hearts. We should sincerely love him, worship him, and serve him. Therefore, Christianity is not about doing business with God but about marrying him. The church's union with Christ is described as a spiritual marriage, and this marriage is a vivid portrayal of the intimate fellowship between God and believers. In this sacred union, Christ is the husband who in love gives his life for his church, and the church is the bride who willingly obeys him.

We are not only drawn by God's love but even more so by God himself. "Draw me after you; let us run" (Song 1:4). Of course, God's love is inseparable from God himself because God is love. But God is not just love—he is also holiness, righteousness, goodness, wisdom, etc. We are deeply drawn by the perfect, glorious, and abundant divine beauty of God himself.

"The first foundation of a true love to God, is that whereby he is in himself lovely, or worthy to be loved, or the supreme loveliness of his nature…what chiefly renders God lovely, and must undoubtedly be the chief ground of true love, is his excellency…but how can a man truly and rightly love God, without loving him for that excellency in him, which is the foundation of all that is in any manner of respect good or desirable in him? They whose affection to God is founded first on his profitableness to them, their affection begins at the wrong end; they regard God only for the utmost limit of the stream of divine good, where it touches them, and reaches their interest; and have no respect to that infinite glory of God's nature, which is the original good, and the true fountain of all good, the first fountain of all loveliness of every kind, and so the first foundation of all true love."[21]

Therefore, in our spiritual lives, we really need to deeply examine our hearts—"Do I really love God? Or do I just want to use God?"

One way to determine whether we are loving God or just using him in our hearts is to reflect on our prayer life. What is the main content of our prayers? What do we often ignore in our prayers? Are our prayers more about obtaining God himself or about him giving us what we want? If our prayers are more about worship, gratitude, and obedience, if we often pray about the kingdom of God and his righteousness, then we are truly living in fellowship with God. On the contrary, if our prayers are basically about asking God to "pay up" (such as asking him to make us healthy, to make our work go smoothly, to help us find the right spouse, to help our family get along, etc.), then we should take heed and repent.

Fellowship with God, Not Rigorous Spiritual Discipline

We must admit that a Christian's spiritual life sometimes stagnates — our life lacks passion and joy; we do experience "miracles" but only spiritual dryness day after day. There may be many causes for such spiritual stagnation, but one important cause is a distorted knowledge of God. We may think of God as a distant traveler who is far away from us. We think that God, most of the time, just does what God does, and man does what man does, and only occasionally do the two cross paths. Our spiritual life then amounts to working hard to understand the Bible to find the laws and rules that God wants man to obey, and then working hard to obey them (e.g. Bible reading, prayer, devotions, good works, etc.).

I have heard some Christians say, "Don't tell me so much about God. Just tell me what to do." This legalistic way of living that lacks fellowship with God will inevitably lead to spiritual dryness. We can only experience continued renewal and vitality in our spiritual lives if we experience genuine fellowship with God, if the true and living triune God is continually before our eyes.

Therefore, repentance is not just about feeling sadness at the fact that God will punish us for our sins. It is more about feeling sorrow and remorse at the fact that my sin is preventing me from experiencing intimate fellowship with a holy God. Believing in Jesus does not just mean praying the sinner's prayer with someone or reciting the Apostle's Creed. It means turning away from oneself to God, facing Christ, following Christ, and walking with Christ.

Professor Yu Daxin has a wonderful summary of Luther's views on faith: "Faith for Luther is not a confession of some creed but rather an experience of being captured by God and brought into a relationship with him. The faith of man first and foremost begins with the faithfulness of God. God first, of his own accord, extends grace to man and invites man into a relationship with him. Faith is responding to this grace, being reconciled to God, and living in this grace. Faith, therefore, is experiencing fellowship with God."[22] In a religion based on fellowship with God, sanctification is not pursued in order to seek favors from God through our own moral accomplishments but rather because the believer is drawn by God's perfect holiness and beauty. He longs to be like God, to draw close to him, to have fellowship with him. He desires that his life would manifest the holiness and glory of the triune God.

Bible reading, prayer, worship, and fellowship with other Christians are all opportunities for a believer to experience fellowship with the triune God.

Reading the Bible is not just about seeing what God said in ancient times to ancient people. It is more about listening to God speaking to me every day. "I rise before dawn and cry for help; I hope in your words. My eyes are awake before the watches of the night, that I may meditate on your promise" (Ps. 119:147–148). "Today, if you hear his voice…" (Ps. 95:7b).

Prayer is not talking to the air, nor is it a routine report or request. It is an intimate conversation with our heavenly Father anytime and anywhere. It is praise and gratitude from the depths of our hearts, a kind of childlike reliance on and appeal to God. In prayer, the children of God come to seek and to see the face of God. "Your face, Lord, do I seek" (Ps. 27:8b). Speaking about seeking God's face in prayer, John Owen says: "The spiritual intense fixation of the mind, by contemplation on God in Christ, until the soul be as it were swallowed up in admiration and delight, and being brought unto utter loss through the infiniteness of those excellencies which it doth admire and adore, it returns again into its own debasements…are things to be aimed at in prayer, and which, through the riches of divine condescension, are frequently enjoyed."[23]

When we experience fellowship with God, we no longer focus on our own feelings in worship. We no longer only focus on the order of worship. We no longer only focus on what everyone is doing or on the atmosphere. Rather, we come together with the resurrected Christ to his holy mountain to give glory and praise to the triune God. In this moment, we see no one but the Lord (Heb. 12:22–24). "When we worship we find that our love for God deepens and the hold that other things have on us loosens. When we worship we find that it changes what we want: we want God and we want to please him more than we want and desire other things."[24]

True fellowship with God will also inevitably lead to true fellowship with man. The church is not just a club where people help and love each other. It is a community of shared life in which people are united to one another in Christ their head. They love, accept, exhort, and unite with one another in the love of God. They bear each other's burdens and share in each other's blessings (Acts 2:42–46, 4:23–35, Phil. 1:5). They build each other up in love (Eph. 4:16).

Fellowship with God, Not Idolatry

It is not only difficult for non-Christians to avoid the snares of idolatry. Christians also, intentionally or unintentionally, often leave their faithful God and flee to the embrace of an idol. "For my people have committed two evils: they have forsaken me, the fountain of living waters, and hewed out cisterns for themselves, broken cisterns that can hold no water" (Jer. 2:13). Even though believers do not often worship physical, tangible idols in a blatant way, we may nevertheless treat some people or things as more important than God himself and try to find satisfaction in them. Those people or things become real gods to us, even though we may not call them "gods." "An idol can be a physical object, a property, a person, an activity, a role, an institution, a hope, an image, an idea, a pleasure, a hero."[25]

But an idol will never bring true satisfaction and joy. King Solomon had the power, wealth, wisdom, wives, and concubines that many men dream of, but he finally admitted that none of these things could bring him real, long-term satisfaction. "Then I considered all that my hands had done and the toil I had expended in doing it, and behold, all was vanity and a striving after wind, and there was nothing to be gained under the sun" (Eccles. 2:11). On the contrary, idol worship fosters feelings of emptiness. When the temporary satisfaction provided by idols vanishes, an even stronger sense of emptiness returns. "Jesus said to her, 'Everyone who drinks of this water will be thirsty again'" (John 4:13). We try to satisfy these inner longings through different idols. If one doesn't work, we replace it with another; if one time doesn't work, we try doing it a few times. We put our hope in the next time or the next thing—"Maybe if I do it just one more time I will be satisfied and my life will be complete." But these attempts repeatedly fail to meet our expectations, and the vicious cycle continues. Idolatry then becomes a snare for us and a source of sorrow. "The sorrows of those who run after another god shall multiply" (Ps. 16:4a).

As people created in the image of God, we are living beings with souls, and souls have deep longings that idols cannot satisfy. We can only be truly satisfied if we truly know and worship God. People and things cannot truly satisfy our hearts but only the triune God. Only the Lord who created our souls can satisfy the desires of our hearts. Just as a child cannot ultimately find satisfaction in toys but only in resting in his mother's arms, Augustine says, "You have made us for Yourself, and our hearts are restless until they rest in You."[26] When the Holy Spirit like a spotlight reveals the glory of God to us, we are drawn to God. All of our idols lose their luster in the light of God's holy glory, and they are revealed to be the false, ugly things that they truly are. When a person comes to truly understand the grace and glory of God, he obtains the power to overcome bondage to all kinds of sins, including bondage to food, women, wealth, and power, and finds true satisfaction and freedom in Christ. Every day the Holy Spirit leads us to continually repent, to trust and obey God, and to experience intimate fellowship with him. The Spirit becomes within us an endless spring (John 4:14, 7:37-39). When we are in fellowship with God, we are in fellowship with the source of life, with the source of glory and abundance and love and joy. Therefore, as people made in the image of God, our supreme satisfaction and joy is knowing God and being brought into fellowship with him (1 John 1:3-4). This is also the fundamental purpose for which we were created: "Man's chief end is to glorify God and to enjoy him forever."[27]

What is amazing is that when we obtain foundational freedom and satisfaction in the triune God, we are also enabled to enjoy the various, good blessings of God with a grateful and joyful heart without treating God's blessings as idols. As the Spirit and the truth guide us, we can approprately use and enjoy God's blessings without overstepping boundaries, just like the freedom that Paul obtained in the Lord: "'All things are lawful for me,' but I will not be enslaved by anything" (1 Cor. 6:12b). Even when God, according to his sovereign will and good purposes, causes us to experience various kinds of poverty, suffering, and persecution in our lives, we are still able to experience joy and satisfaction that are inexpressible and full of glory (1 Pet. 1:8). This shows that our satisfaction and joy are in

God alone. "Though the fig tree should not blossom, nor fruit be on the vines, the produce of the olive fail and the fields yield no food, the flock be cut off from the fold and there be no herd in the stalls, yet I will rejoice in the Lord; I will take joy in the God of my salvation" (Hab. 3:17–18).

Conclusion

The God in whom we believe is not a collection of inanimate matter or a set of laws, nor is he a lonely and cold tyrant or dictator. We believe in the triune God, who experiences mutual love within himself, who out of this abundant love created all things, and who creates man in his own image so that humanity might imitate his love and love him with all their heart and soul and strength and love their neighbor as themselves.

Therefore, when we know this loving and glorious triune God and understand his unique creation and redemptive love, we can trust, worship, love, enjoy, and serve God more deeply in reverence and gratitude. When we know the triune God, we can drink true love and supreme joy from this fountain of life. We can feel affection for him and live righteous lives through him. Our faith, then, is not just a theory or doctrine but a living love for God and for the world.

As Michael Reeves puts it, "In the triune God is the love behind all love, the life behind all life, the music behind all music, the beauty behind all beauty and the joy behind all joy. In other words, in the triune God is a God we can heartily enjoy—and enjoy in and through his creation."[28]

James Qin pastored a house church in a Chinese city for 8 years before going to seminary. Since graduating he has planted another church.

Further Reflection:

- Qin gives a brief overview of the entire Bible as a story of God's pursuit of a restored relationship with man. Is this the image of God you were taught? How does this enrich our typical understanding of making a "decision" for Christ?

- Both Chinese and Western culture can push us toward a transactional or legalistic relationship with God. Are the Chinese cultural examples he gives similar or different to what we might experience in the West? What do we need to push back on or counteract in our own culture?

- This chapter touches on the experiential and relational aspect of sanctification, which was discussed in the previous chapter. Write a brief summary, or even a gospel presentation, based on these two Chinese authors' view of becoming a Christian.

3

The Gospel of Grace Alone

Li Ye

The gospel is the core of the Christian faith. A Christian is one who believes the gospel. But this truth that is commonly taken for granted is not necessarily reflected in the lives of individual Christians or church communities. That is to say, the gospel is not significantly influencing the lives of individual Christians or church communities. It has not become the center of their lives or the driving force behind their ministries.

In the end, this is usually the result of an inadequate or distorted understanding of the gospel. Problems with the fruit are often due to problems with the root. Similarly, problems with external behavior are often due to distorted knowledge. As R.C. Sproul says, "The gospel of Jesus Christ is always at risk of distortion. It became distorted in the centuries leading up to the Protestant Reformation in the sixteenth century. It became distorted at innumerable other points of church history, and it is often distorted today. This is why Martin Luther said the gospel must be defended in every generation. It is the center point of attack by the forces of evil. They know that if they can get rid of the gospel, they can get rid of Christianity."[29]

Indeed, every generation must defend the gospel and protect the seeds of orthodox Christianity. This was true during the Protestant Reformation, and it is also true today. If the Protestant Reformation was about rediscoering the gospel, then such "rediscovery" needs to take place continually throughout every generation and in the life of every Christian. Furthermore, unless the gospel is continually found in the church and correctly preached and taught, the church cannot experience a true revival, nor can it serve the generation in which it exists or bear a glorious testimony for the sake of God's name. What's even more frightening, if we are not preaching the true gospel, then we are preaching a false one. We are preaching not the gospel but a curse.

Whether Christianity flourishes or fades, whether the Church rises or falls, is determined by and dependent on the gospel. Drawing from various experiences in pastoral ministry over the past few years, I will attempt in this article to increase our knowledge and understanding of the gospel and to answer the question of how this knowledge and uderstanding affects our preaching of the gospel and how we ought to preach this unparalleled gospel of grace.

Li Ye

The Content of the Gospel

The Gospel Is Good News

The gospel is news, and it is good news. The gospel is not a good suggestion about what we should do. It is good news that proclaims what God has done for us.

The Gospel Is to Be Proclaimed

The gospel is good news proclaiming or announcing that someone has been rescued from danger. D.A. Carson draws this conclusion from a thorough study of gospel-related words: "Because the gospel is news, good news... it is to be announced; that is what one does with news. The essential heraldic element in preaching is bound up with the fact that the core message is not a code of ethics to be debated, still less a list of aphorisms to be admired and pondered, and certainly not a systematic theology to be outlined and schematized. Though it properly grounds ethics, aphorisms, and systematics, it is none of these three: it is news, good news, and therefore must be publicly announced."[30]

The Gospel Is of Grace

The gospel is good news that is external to us and that proclaims what God has done for us. We are just messengers of the gospel, and a messenger's job is simply to report a message, just as Pheidippides, the pioneer of the marathon competition and messenger during the Grco-Persian Wars, did not announce what he had done but rather the victory that the Athenians had won.

The gospel is the news that Christ has accomplished salvation in history—and all because of God's grace. "Nothing in my hands I bring, simply to thy cross I cling." As that beloved "big pastor"[31] says, the heart of salvation is "grace alone." If salvation is entirely of the Lord and not because of any meritorious works of my own, then the mystery of the gospel is that a failed man has been saved by God's unfailing grace through the death and resurrection of Christ.

The Heart of the Gospel Is Jesus Christ

The gospel is "the gospel of Jesus Christ, the Son of God" (Mark 1:1). This good news is about a person. It is about the incarnate Jesus Christ. In short, the gospel is what God has done in history—the good news that God saved the world through his Son. Therefore, he is the historical fulfillment of all that God promised through the prophets in Scripture. He is the realization of the hopes of all generations.

As D.A. Carson says, "As we have seen, [the gospel is] the gospel of God regarding his Son (Rom. 1). There is no conflict between these two designations ("Jesus of Nazareth, the King of the Jews" [John 19:19]), and both drive us to focus on Jesus Christ, the Son of God, the King, whose utterly extraordinary mission was to die the odious death of an accursed wretch, in fulfillment of Old Testament patterns and pictures and prophecies of sacrifice. The good news that focuses on Jesus and his cross-work was anticipated, according to Paul, two millennia earlier in the promises given to Abraham (Gal. 3:8), and repeatedly promised in the Scriptures (Rom. 1:2)."[32]

Therefore, the gospel is not everything. The heart of the gospel is Jesus Christ. Christianity is Christ.

The core and essence of the gospel concerns the person and work of Jesus Christ—who he is and what he has done. Jesus is the Christ, the Son of the living God. He came down in the flesh, was sacrificed on the cross, rose from the dead, ascended into heaven, and he will return again as King. Every stage of Christ's life is the foundation of our salvation. Through him we obtain the benefits of salvation—we are born again, justified, sanctified, and made children of God; we enter the kingdom of the beloved Son, God's family, and are united to Christ; we obtain newness of life, victory over sin, and future glory.

What exactly is the gospel? S.E. Wang provides a comprehensive summary of the gospel: the gospel is that God, through the incarnation, death, resurrection, and ascension of Jesus Christ, fulfilled his promise of salvation and inaugurated the coming and reign of his eschatological kingdom. In Jesus Christ, the second Adam, God cleanses man of his sin, makes him born again, and restores the image of God in him and his kingship over creation. Christ will come again to complete God's redemptive work that all glory might be given to God.[33] This definition succinctly describes the person and work of Jesus Christ and displays the core elements of the gospel—Jesus's incarnation, death, resurrection, judgment, and reign.

The Gospel Is Rooted in Biblical Revelation

The gospel does not begin in the four Gospels. The gospel is an ancient religion that begins in Genesis. Even though we cannot consider every teaching in the Bible to be the gospel, all biblical doctrine is necessary background for understanding the gospel.[34]

In other words, the gospel and the biblical narratives are closely connected. We cannot understand the gospel apart from the biblical narratives. The gospel is a story, and the Bible as a whole is a big story. Every part of the Bible is telling this story. This story speaks to our most basic desires and deepest hopes. The structure of this story is creation, depravity, redemption, and consummation. The story of the Bible is the story of the gospel, the story of God—and it is our story.

The Focus of the Gospel

The Gospel Is Not Everything

In his helpful segment on Gospel Theology in the book *Center Church*, Tim Keller discusses three aspects of gospel theology:[35]

- **"The gospel is not everything."** The core and essence of the gospel is about who Christ is and what he has done.

- **"The gospel is not a simple thing."** The meaning of

"gospel" is very rich. Much popular "gospel terminology" distills the gospel into a few core principles, often at the cost of richness and accuracy. All of Scripture speaks about the gospel and points to Christ. The Bible is a gospel drama.

- **"The gospel affects everything."** Keller says that the gospel is not the ABCs of Christianity but the A to Z of Christianity. It speaks into every aspect of the life of believers and of the church. We must not think that the gospel is only about salvation and that our growth after conversion depends on our own numerous efforts. The gospel is not just a door but a path that we must walk down every day. The gospel is the power of God, and it not only brings us salvation and justification but the transformation and renewal of sanctification. The gospel is both how we are saved and how we transformed. The gospel changes everything!

Both Christians and unbelievers need the message of the gospel. The gospel is the only way out of this lost and broken world. No ministry of the church should ever, at any time, deviate from this gospel-focus. Our ministries ought to be driven and shaped by the gospel. The gospel is at the center of all ministry.

The Gospel is Not Moralism or Liberalism

Keller also speaks about "two thieves" or errors that can rob the gospel of its power.[36] One is moralism and the other is relativism. These pose a great threat to the gospel. All error and confusion in the church is a result of an incorrect understanding and application of the gospel.

1. Moralism: If you act rightly, you will be loved. (Rom. 2:1–3:8)

2. Liberalism: Reject God and live according to your own desires. (Rom. 1:18–32)

3. Gospel: Those who receive grace will obey.

These appear to be three different ways of living, but they are actually only two beliefs. The gospel points to God's salvation and grace, while moralism and liberalism amount to us saving ourselves—we become our own saviors. Moralism relies on one's own efforts to do good. We purchase God's love with our moral accomplishments that we achieve by obeying his Law. Liberalism completely rejects God as savior. It promotes living according to one's own ideas and pushes God out of his world. Moralism and liberalism are two enemies of the gospel.

Moralism has no grace or forgiveness, nor does it produce love and worship. In the eyes of moralists, faith is reduced to a transaction—we exchange our own righteousness for God's acceptance. If God's love depends on our performance, then we must face a painful and troubling question: How much is "enough" to a holy God? Moralism urges people to diligently serve God, but we will experience great anguish as we try to do so because our service is not out of love for God. It will lead to bitterness and resentment. As Geerhardus Vos says, "Legalism lacks the supreme sense of worship. It obeys but it does not adore."[37]

Moreover, moralism provides no hope, no escape, and no comfort—because it does not accept failures or morally deficient people. Its most fatal flaw is a lack of grace. It does not know the sweetness of God's free, atoning forgiveness or the rest found in Christ's righteousness. The gospel of moralism lacks the grace necessary to save oneself from corruption. Ask yourself: Who is not a moral failure before a holy and righteous God? According to the Bible, we are all sinners who fall short of the glory of God (Rom. 3:23).

Liberalism exalts grace and freedom, but it does not know the holy, just, and good law of God. Love without law is empty love because it claims that God (if there is a God) accepts us and loves us no matter what we do. Liberalism provides cheap grace, a grace through which you forgive yourself. Liberalism believes in freedom. This freedom is the spirit of our post-modern age, and it has plundered the minds and hearts of many. These are men who "put their trust in a God without wrath who brings men without sin into a kingdom without judgment through the ministrations of a Christ without a Cross."[38]

The gospel opposes moralism and liberalism because they repudiate God's salvation and reject Christ and his cross. Both of these ideologies are sins. They essentially want man to redeem himself and to become his own lord.

Moralism does not recognize the holiness and justice of God. As a result, we do not realize that we are more evil and deficient than we think. Liberalism does not recognize God's transcendent and generous love, and as a result we do not realize that we can be more easily accepted and loved than we imagine. Grace turns everything upside down: the self-righteous are condemned, and the self-condemned are made righteous. The gospel is that we are sinners who have received grace.

Pastor Wang Yi summarizes the gospel even better: "The gospel destroys our pride, for it says that the Son of God had to die for us. There is no other way we can be saved than by the Son of God shedding his blood for us. The gospel also destroys our fear, for when we were enemies of God, he laid down his life for us. This means that, from now on, no enemy can defeat us, and no failure can take away the love that we have received."

The Supremacy of Grace

Man was created as a religious being. He is a worshiper by nature. Man is always worshipping something, every minute of every day. However, because of sin, as Calvin says, the heart has become an idol factory. We are enslaved to idols. Idol worship destroys our lives and causes us to worship and serve the creature rather than the Creator. Like the prodigal son, we have lost our home and are wandering aimlessly away from home. All of humanity is a group of wanderers who want to return home. We are in the same miserable predicament as the prodigal son. Unless God seeks us, we cannot restore our relationship with him.

If the gospel is all of grace, then this means that no one can please God by relying on himself. Grace cuts us to the heart. The gospel is often offensive. Self-righteous sinners hate the cross. It is a stumbling block to many (Gal. 5:11). For the cross tells people that they cannot do anything to earn their salvation. It cannot accommodate human toil and effort. It declares that all human efforts to earn salvation have utterly failed. The gospel proclaims the powerlessness of man and the power of God.

Grace and truth came to us through the incarnation of Jesus Christ (John 1:14). Christianity is unique in that God comes to us of his own accord to bring us back to himself. We are saved and made children of God by relying solely on the grace of God. This grace is to be received. It originates outside of us. It is given to us by Christ. He was crucified on our behalf and paid the debt for our sin.

John Piper has written many books, one of which is titled *The Legacy of Sovereign Joy*. It is subtitled *God's Triumphant Grace in the Lives of Augustine, Luther, and Calvin*. The introduction is titled "Savoring the Sovereignty of Grace in the Lives of Flawed Saints." In the book, he says that Augustine, Luther, and Calvin were flawed human beings but that they had one thing in common—they experienced, and then built their lives and ministries on, the reality of God's omnipotent grace. Each of them confessed openly that the essence of experiential Christianity is the glorious triumph of grace over the guilty impotence of man.[39]

The gospel is the amazing grace of God to save lost sinners. Liberalism does not understand grace. Moralism has no grace. We live in a culture, a barren desert, in which there is no grace. The church has been entrusted with the responsibility of continually preaching the gospel of grace to this generation and culture.

Preaching the Gospel

We not only believe the gospel but have been entrusted with preaching it, and how we preach is determined by the nature and substance of the gospel itself.

The Gospel Is Declarative and Transformative News

The gospel is a public declaration for the whole world. It is also the power of God, and it brings about salvation and transformation. The gospel is the foundation and source of all our actions, both inside and outside the church, both individually and corporately.

D.A. Carson has said that the gospel must be presented as intellectual truth that can be believed and obeyed. But this gospel is never merely intellectual; it must be preached, taught, and lived out in the church as the glorious gospel of our beloved savior.

The church must go out and proclaim the gospel to unbelievers and convert them. Then it must gather these converts together and teach and pastor them with the gospel so that the gospel might renew and transform their whole lives. They must "live out" the gospel.

74

Preaching Is Christ-centered

The gospel is called "the gospel of Jesus Christ." Christ is the heart of the gospel. To preach the heart of the gospel is to preach Christ, to preach his identity and his offices. Gospel preaching must never deviate from this center. The identity and offices of Christ are systematic-theological perspectives on Christ. When we preach the gospel we can adopt these redemptive-historical or systematic-theological perspectives.

As Douglas Moo says, "God's work in Christ is the center of history, the point from which both past and future must be understood. The cross and resurrection of Christ are both the fulfillment of the Old Testament and the basis and anticipation of final glory. With Christ as the climax of history, then, history can be divided into two 'eras,' or 'aeons,' each with its own founder—Adam and Christ, respectively—and each with its own ruling powers—sin, the law, flesh, and death on the one hand; righteousness, grace, the Spirit, and life on the other. All people start out in the 'old era' by virtue of particpation in the act by which it was founded—the sin of Adam (Rom. 5:12, 18–19). But one can be transferred into the 'new era' by becoming joined to Christ, the founder of that era, thereby participating in the acts through which that era came into being—Christ's death, burial, and resurrection (Rom. 6:1–6)."[40]

Each part of Christ's life is the foundation and substance of our salvation. To preach the gospel is to preach the incarnation of Christ, his death and resurrection, his judgment and sovereignty, and the benefits of salvation that these all bring. Moreover, to preach the gospel is to call people to respond to the gospel with repentance and faith. D.A. Carson says that the gospel is the joyous news that is the foundation of our repentance and belief. Similarly Paul Tripp teaches that the gospel is the fertile soil in which true repentance grows. The promises of the gospel make me willing to confront my sins, and they also give me the strength to turn from my sins. In Christ, we can find real hope for real transformation. This is the foundation of repentance.

Preaching the Gospel from All of Scripture

Scripture testifies about Jesus Christ, and all of Scripture proclaims the gospel. We want to preach Christ and his gospel from every passage in the Bible. The Mosaic Law can reveal the message of grace. The Bible similarly teaches us through poetry, proverbs, history, and letters. We must use different methods to help us see this unparalleled gospel in different types of Scripture, to see this single thread that runs throughout all of its pages—and this thread is Christ. We must be Christ-centered and gospel -centered.

Preaching the Gospel with the Redemptive-Historical Method

I mentioned earlier that the entire Bible is a gospel narrative, a story about Jesus Christ, a story about how

Christ saved us. The center of this story is Christ. It is his story. And there are four chapters to this story:

1. Creation: The Initial Chorus of the Cosmos

This story does not begin with us but with the creation of God. God's creation was not necessary because of some lack in himself—he is completely self-sufficient. His creation was an overflow of his perfection, of his love, goodness, and glory. The personal God, infinite, omnipotent, and eternal, created this beautiful universe out of love, and the history of this universe began with a garden. God created humans in his own image and likeness and gave them dignity and glory. We were made in order to glorify, worship, serve, and enjoy God.

When our thinking is rooted in God's creation, it helps us to affirm those cultural hopes that are consistent with the beliefs and values of Scripture while also challenging those things that are not consistent with the beliefs and values of Scripture. We must show people that Christ alone is all we long and hope for. We must invite and draw people to Christ by means of these cultural hopes (such as a longing for recognition, acceptance, belonging, a sense of value, safety, etc.). As Tim Keller says, "To reach people gospel preachers must challenge the culture's story at points of confrontation and finally retell the culture's story, as it were, revealing how its deepest aspirations for good can be fulfilled only by Christ."[41]

2. Fall: The Miserable Plight of Sinners

God created us to worship him, love him, and serve him. But instead of obeying and serving him out of gratitude and joy, man in his sin rebelled against God. All of man's problems stem from this great rebellion recorded in Genesis 3. Man ruins his own life because of sin. Man's rebellion also causes the whole world to fall into the darkness and chaos of sin. Our predicament is that we have rebelled against God and incurred his wrath and judgment. We were driven out of paradise and have become residents of the "city of destruction" where we experience toil, worry, disease, sorrow, and death (Gen. 3:16–19).

Sin continually affects our lives so that we become ungodly. We rebel against the kingdom of God and try to establish our own kingdom. We fight against God and want to become God ourselves. When we do not worship the Creator, we worship and serve the creation and find our life, identity, value, meaning and happiness in it. All kinds of things, visible and invisible, replace God and became our "idols." Soon, these idols enslave us and take control of our lives and hearts, causing us to greatly rebel against the holiness and justice of God. The shadow of death hangs over our lives.

In their natural, corrupt state, sinners are objects of God's wrath. We must clearly proclaim the lostness and hopelessness of man. This is not a preaching technique. It is the real predicament of man, our true, post-fallen plight. Sinners need to feel this sense of crisis and understand that they are hopeless, that they are at a dead end. The problem that sinners have is not that they are hopeless but that they are not hopeless enough—they do not feel a need for the gospel. We must help them to repeatedly see and experience the holiness and justice of God so that they might discern, confess, and feel just how broken their lives are and how great their sin is so that we might awaken within them a desire for salvation and a need for a savior.

Luther believed that the primary goal of the preacher was to shatter self-confidence in the audience and to drive them to despair. Once the preaching of the law has driven men to despair, the job of the minister is then to declare the gospel and point them to Christ.[42]

3. Redemption: The Display of God's Mercy

When the Law is properly preached and man sees God's all-surpassing glory and holiness and consequently realizes how short he has fallen of the glory of God and what disastrous consequences he faces because of this, only then will he, like Christian in Pilgrim's Progress, cry out in despair: "What shall I do?"

The church has been instructed to preach the comfort and hope of the gospel to these desperate sinners. "Christ Jesus came into the world to save sinners" (1 Tim. 1:15). Just as every story has a hero, the hero of the gospel story is Jesus Christ. Throughout all of human history, man has been looking for a hero to be their savior, their redeemer, their liberator, to save man from the bondage and judgment of sin and to restore to the world the beauty it once had.

The Lord Jesus became flesh and came to this world

not to judge it but to save it. He came full of grace and truth. He died on the cross in the place of his elect according to the Scriptures, and on the third day he rose from the dead in accordance with the Scriptures, conquering sin, death, and hell.

4. Consummation: The Renewal of All Creation

The gospel is a gospel of redemption that saves individual souls. But the gospel is also universal. When Christ returns, God's grace will restore to nature the beauty it once had. When the world was created, it began as a garden, and when it is redeemed and consummated, it will be a garden city with roots—the City of God. God will renew all things (Rev. 21:5). Everything that was lost and broken and corrupted by the Fall will be corrected, restored, and healed through redemption. We will be with God forever in that new heaven and new earth, where we will enjoy new and eternal life.

Cornelius Plantinga says, "The coming of the kingdom of God represents a final state of cosmic redemption, in which God and God's creatures dwell together in harmony and righteousness. It represents shalom—universal flourishing, wholeness, and delight…On the one hand, we need to avoid triumphalism, the prideful view that we Christians will fully succeed in transforming all or much of culture…On the other hand, we need to avoid the despairing tendency to write the world off and to remove ourselves to an island of like-minded Christians. The world, after all, belongs to God and is in the process of being redeemed by God. God's plan is to gather up all things in Christ (Eph 1:9–10). Christians have been invited to live beyond triumphalism and despair, spending ourselves for a cause we firmly believe will win in the end. In a vision lovely enough to break a person's heart, John shows us in Revelation 21 that heaven comes to us and renews this world."[43]

Conclusion

This is the gospel of grace that we confess, and it is the gospel that we preach—the gospel that God reveals, that Christ accomplishes, and that the Spirit applies to every Christian and church community. It was the rediscovery of the gospel that gave rise to the Protestant Reformation and that gave it lasting momentum and caused it to bear fruit. It was the gospel that launched the Protestant Reformation. May this gospel of grace alone launch a reformation—a gospel revolution—in this generation, both in the church and in the lives of individual Christians. May the gospel subvert us and renew us. We have been captured and commandeered by this gospel. We have been called to be witnesses and laborers of this gospel. We have been called to testify to the work of God in history and to the work of his gospel in our lives and in our church communities. And we have been called to look forward to the glorious second coming of Jesus Christ!

Li Ye was called to pastor an urban house church in a city in the southwest of China in 2000, and has been serving there ever since.

Further Reflection:

- The author argues that every generation must rediscover the gospel, and whether the church rises or falls depends on it. How is the gospel being lost in our current generation? How would taking this seriously change your church's approach to ministry?

- The author summarizes many Western pastors and theologians on the gospel. What surprises you about the sources he draws from? Which of these ideas has most impacted your understanding of the gospel?

- What strategies does he offer to preach the gospel? How do they serve to help us preserve, defend, or rediscover the gospel?

4

The Gospel Restores the Order of God

Brian Li

Many pastors and theologians define the gospel according to systematic theology. It is easy to view the gospel as the first step into a personalized form of Christianity and to overlook its continuing, communal, dynamic nature. The gospel has unfortunately become perceived as a one-time doctrinal statement to be understood. It has become a personal choice and a static process. This has caused church congregations to fall into the error of thinking that we rely on Christ to become Christian, and we rely on ourselves to live out the Christian life. If our original understanding of the gospel is distorted, our spiritual disciplines and theological reflections will not substantially transform us.

We must understand the Bible from a biblical perspective.

The Biblical Definition of the Gospel

The Gospel Is Good News

The original word for "gospel" in the New Testament is "euangelion." The first half of this word means "good" or "happy," and the second half means "message" or "news." Simply put, the gospel is good news. We see in the Gospel of Luke how the gospel was proclaimed: "And the angel said to them, 'Fear not, for behold, I bring you good news of great joy that will be for all the people. For unto you is born this day in the city of David a Savior, who is Christ the Lord'" (Luke 2:10–11). The Bible also records that those shepherds who heard this good news also spread it. As we can see, the gospel is good news that is joyfully proclaimed by messengers and continually spread by others.

The gospel must not only be proclaimed but also explained. In the Bible, the gospel is also called the "gospel of the kingdom of heaven" and the "gospel of the kingdom of God." When the New Testament authors recorded the gospel of Jesus Christ, they summarized it as the good news of the kingdom of God. In other words, the gospel that Jesus Christ preached is rooted in the kingdom of God. The good news of the kingdom of God is also in the Old Testament. The announcement of the angels in Luke 2:10–11 mentions the fulfillment of Old Testament prophecies.

A Three-Point Outline of the Gospel

How should we express the gospel? What are its core

elements?

Tim Keller summarizes Simon Gathercole's three-point outline from the letters of Paul as follows:

"He writes that for Paul the good news was, first, that Jesus is the promised messianic King and Son of God come to earth as a servant, in human form (Rom. 1:3-4; Phil. 2:5–11). Second, by his death and resurrection, Jesus atoned for our sin and secured our justification by grace, not by our works (1 Cor. 15:3, 9–10). Third, on the cross Jesus broke the dominion of sin and evil over us (Col. 2:13–15), and at his return he will complete what he began by the renewal of the entire material creation and the resurrection of our bodies (Rom. 8:18–23)."

The gospel, therefore, focuses on these three things: Jesus Christ's incarnation, resurrection from the dead, and glorious second coming.

This means that the gospel is not about everything. It is about who Jesus Christ is and what he has done for us. It is about how our relationship with God is restored through the work of Christ. At the same time, Christians' understanding of the gospel must be based on the teachings of the Bible as revealed to us by God.

The kingdom of God was part of God's original design for mankind. As followers of Jesus Christ, we must understand this good news. The kingdom of God began when the world was created, and it will last until the world ends. The Bible not only prepares us for the sake of Christ's work but also explains the meaning of this work in detail.

Understanding the Order of God

I would like to attempt to present the gospel by surveying the grand narrative of Scripture, tracing the theme of the "order of God."

In the Chinese urban church planting movement over the past few years, I have found that some urban pastors are trying to put "new wine into old wineskins." Treating gospel theology as an effective method, they attempted to use a corresponding philosophy of ministry to govern the church, and by this they hope to bring about revival in the church.

The gospel is not a set of methods. The gospel causes subversive transformation. It grants new life to men, life that is ordered completely contrary to this fallen world. The gospel reorders our lives and our communities. The Bible often tells us to live "in Christ" and to "live according to the gospel." Through Christ, by the mercy of God, the gospel allows us to live once again according to the righteous and holy order of God, and this order is created through the power and wisdom of a gracious God.

If we do not live according to the order established by God, we are not living according to the gospel. Only those who live lives reordered by the gospel can bring revival to the church.

Understanding Order

In order to help us understand the concept of "order," let us first look at the cosmic realm outside of earth. The realm of outer space is ordered. The law by which the various planets and galaxies move is called Newton's "law of universal gravitation." Behind this law are the powerful and wise workings of God. Even though you cannot see this, the Bible tells us about it. Genesis 1:16–17 says that God not only made the sun and the moon but also placed the stars in the sky. God appointed celestial bodies as administrators to operate according to these cosmic laws. This is "order."

At the end of the world, before the second coming of Jesus Christ, there will be a sign in the heavens (Matt. 24:29–30). This sign is described in detail in Rev. 6:12–17. When the sixth seal is opened, the celestial bodies will undergo a dramatic change—the stars will fall from heaven. This is "disorder."

In the same way, God appointed man—the image of God—to be his administrators on earth, to govern the earth according to his order and to turn it into the glorious kingdom of God. But man shirked his responsibility from God. As a result, man threw God's entire kingdom out of order and brought death upon himself. This is the result of a disordered life.

But in his mercy and kindness, God worked salvation. How did he restore order to man's life and to his kingdom through Jesus Christ?

Let us look at how the gospel subverts this fallen world and brings us back to the eternal will and order of God. May the Lord give us a spirit of wisdom and of revelation, having the eyes of our hearts enlightened, that we may see and understand the beauty of the gospel. May we pastors truly understand the gospel, eagerly embrace it, make it the driving force of our lives, and let it shape the direction of our churches.

The Creation of God's Kingdom

The Bible reveals that God wants to turn the whole earth into his own kingdom. This is his eternal will. In the beginning, God created all things out of a universe that was without form and void. He appointed man as priest and king on earth to expand his kingdom to the ends of the earth. In Revelation 11:15, we see how this world will end: "The kingdom of the world has become the kingdom of our Lord and of his Christ, and he shall reign forever and ever." In the end, Christ will extend God's kingdom throughout the whole earth. This theme of the "kingdom" runs throughout the entire Bible, and it is governed by and operates according to God's established order.

The Order of God

The problem God faced when he first created his kingdom was that it was "formless and void." "Formless" means to have no shape or structure. "Void" means to be empty, to have nothing. God solved this problem of formlessness and emptiness by his wisdom and power, and an orderly world was created.

On the first three days of creation, we can see that God solved the problem of formlessness by means of "separation." On the first day, God established a distinction in the universe between light and darkness. On the second day, he separated the waters below the atmosphere into two halves. On the third day, he established a boundary between land and sea on earth. He created form and structure in heaven and on earth.

On the final three days of creation, we can see that God solved the problem of "emptiness" by means of "filling." In these three days, God created the sun, moon, and stars to fill the universe, birds and fish to fill the sky and sea, and animals and people to fill the land. He created a world full of life. God appointed these creatures with structure to oversee the normal operations of the entire system. He commanded the celestial bodies to oversee the universe (Gen. 1:16–18), and he commanded mankind to oversee the whole earth (Gen. 1:26).

From this we can clearly see how the Bible defines the "order of God." God first establishes a structure; then he fills this structure with created things; then he appoints these creatures as administrators to manage the structure and ensure that it operates smoothly; and finally, he blesses the entire system. This sequence of "frame—fill—manage" displays the wisdom and power of God. The universe is able to function according to this order because behind it, God is upholding all things by his power.

The Elements of the Kingdom

A kingdom primarily consists of four elements: citizens, land, laws, and a development plan. Who does God as king choose to be his citizens? What is the domain and development plan of his kingdom? What laws does it have? Let us explore the kingdom that God has created.

The First Element: Citizens

Man was created in the image of God (Gen. 1:26). Genesis 2:7 records this process in detail: "Then the Lord God formed the man of dust from the ground and breathed into his nostrils the breath of life, and the man became a living creature."

We can see the order of God in the life of man. First, God created a body from the dust of the earth. This is the structure of man. It solved the problem of "formlessness." Then God breathed the breath of life into man's body, filling man with a spirit. This solved the problem of "emptiness." God made man into a living creature with a spirit, and then this body with a soul became animated. The soul is responsible for managing the operations of the body. This is the "order of life"—the body is the vehicle of the soul, and the soul is the administrator of the body.

The most marvelous creative act of God was his giving man a soul and making him a creature with an independent personality. God gave meaning to the inner life of man, exalted meaning that transcended all things in the universe. For man shared in the nature of the Creator of this universe by possessing spiritual traits like wisdom, benevolence, righteousness, and holiness.

As the image of God, man reflected God. God granted dignity and value to man, giving him a sense of glory. This sense of glory caused man to love both himself and others. He was very honest and intimate and was willing to obey God. Man was also God's representative. He was given authority to exercise dominion over the whole earth. Like God, he ruled the earth.

The Second Element: Land

God gave his citizens the land that he created to live in. When the earth was first created, although it was perfect, it was still very primitive (Gen. 2:5–6). In order to transform the whole earth into the kingdom of God, it was necessary to further perfect the order of this kingdom. In the beginning, only the garden of Eden fully displayed the order of God. The garden was a perfect land where God was totally present. It was filled with harmony and order. God gave the garden to Adam and Eve and charged Adam with the responsibility of governing it by "working" and "keeping" it. God desired that his people would live in accordance with his calling on their lives to "be fruitful and multiply and fill the earth and subdue it" in order that the whole earth might achieve the end for which God made it—to become the kingdom of God.

The Third Element: A Development Plan

After creating his kingdom, God's plan was that man would complete the work of "subduing the earth" by obeying the command to "be fruitful and multiply and fill the earth." In human history, only Adam and Eve were created by God. After this, he gave mankind the authority to create men, allowing man and woman to create images of God by means of a sexual union in marriage. Within this marriage relationship, man and woman were to raise up the next generation of priestly kings to serve the great King. And when a child was grown, he was to "leave his father and his mother and hold fast to his wife, and they shall become one flesh." In this way, man was to continue to plant new gardens of Eden.

We can see from this that the garden of Eden was a template given by God—man was to develop the world according to this Edenic order. If man had developed the world according to this pattern, the garden of Eden would have filled the whole earth when he was finished. This was God's will. For God's ultimate goal was that the dwelling place of God's holy people would become the dwelling place of God. "And I heard a loud voice from the throne saying, 'Behold, the dwelling place of God is with man. He will dwell with them, and they will be his people, and God himself will be with them as their God'" (Rev. 21:3). From this we can see that God wanted to create for himself a family. This was the fundamental purpose for which God put mankind on earth.

The Fourth Element: Law

The laws of this kingdom are God's commandments. Citizens of this kingdom must obey God's commandments and live according to the order of life, the order of Eden, and the order of the Kingdom. Man was to maintain this order by following one commandment: "Of the tree of the knowledge of good and evil you shall not eat."

To obey this commandment would result in a life in harmony with the order of God, but to disobey would result in a disordered life.

Satan Subverts the Order of God's Kingdom

As the whole earth was fulfilling God's kingdom plan, a cunning adversary attempted to destroy this plan. He knew that the best way to do so was to cause man to violate God's commandment, thereby bringing disorder to man's life and subverting the order of God's whole kingdom. So Satan plotted, looking for an opportunity to attack, and he found it in the garden of Eden.

The Order of Eden

In Genesis 2, we see that God established order in the garden of Eden by means of work and marriage.

First, man's job was to "work" and "keep" the garden. "Working" the garden involved worshipping and serving God, that is managing the garden according to God's righteous attributes and wisdom. "Keeping" it involved obeying God's commandments, maintaining the garden, and enjoying God's presence and blessing.

Second, God desired Adam and Eve to enter into a beautiful covenant relationship through marriage. Through the husband's leadership and the wife's help, their family was to be run according to God's will. In this covenant union, they were to produce godly descendants and prepare future generations to plant new gardens of Eden when they grew up.

The Order of the Kingdom

We know that in this kingdom development plan, the "order of God" consists of three stages: "frame—fill—manage," and these are all linked together.

First, God established the "order of life." God's Spirit filled man's body, and man, under the Spirit's rule, reflected and represented God.

Next, God established the "order of Eden." He filled the garden with man (the order of life), and appointed him to exercise dominion over it—to work it and keep it and to be fruitful and multiply according to the order of marriage.

Finally, God established the "order of the kingdom." The garden of Eden was to fill the whole earth. Man was to govern the world according to the Edenic order until he finally ruled the whole earth according to the "order of God."

In the order of the kingdom, the "order of life" was the central thing that linked everything together. At the heart of this "order of life" is man's obedience to and trust in God. Man cannot exist independently outside of God. He must view God as the Lord of his life. Through man, God intended to rule the whole earth perfectly and to bring order to his kingdom.

Of course, this all-important "order of life" still had to pass a test. Would the image of God remain faithful to him?

Satan Attacks the Order of Eden

In Genesis 3, we see how the serpent tempts man and

causes him to sin.

First, why does the serpent speak with the woman and not with the man? He is effectively attacking the order of marriage. Within a marriage structure in which the man leads and the woman follows, if the couple wants to make a decision it is the man who must make the decision, not the woman. So the cunning serpent talks to the woman, thus beginning the process of destroying the marriage order.

Second, the serpent's conversation continually focuses on the consequences of eating the forbidden fruit. He begins a process of suppressing God's truth with lies with the goal of tricking man into violating God's commandments, causing him to fail in his duty to keep the garden and consequently destroying the order of life.

The conversation finally reaches a climax when the serpent enticingly tells Eve that if she eats the forbidden fruit she will "be like God." He subverts the order of life and incites man to abandon God. This is an attack on the order of life.

The Failure and Unfaithfulness of Man

We can't help but ask, "What was Adam doing during this whole process?" He had a responsibility to "keep" the garden. In that moment, he ought to have been protecting the order of the garden according to God's word.

First, when the serpent attacked the order of marriage, Adam ought to have used the authority that God gives to men to lead their families. He ought to have immediately forbidden Eve from listening to the lies of the serpent and then forbidden her from taking the forbidden fruit. But he was silent during the entire encounter.

Secondly, when the serpent assaulted the order of work, Adam ought to have remembered the commandment of God: "Of the tree of the knowledge of good and evil you shall not eat." In that moment he ought to have exercised his responsibility as a man to "keep" the garden. He ought to have spoken and declared God's words before Eve and the serpent. He ought to have proclaimed the supremacy of God's word and authoritatively rebuked the serpent's lies. But he neglected this duty.

Finally, when the serpent attacked the order of life, Adam ought to have categorically rejected the serpent's temptation and commanded him to leave. But he believed the lie in his heart. The motivation that ultimately drove Adam and Eve to eat the forbidden fruit was the promise that they would "be like God."

God originally desired to extend his kingdom order throughout the whole earth by means of their faithfulness. But they were unfaithful. They neglected their role as king and priest, betrayed God, and believed Satan. Satan successfully destroyed the Edenic order. God's authority structure was dismantled and the order of God's kingdom subverted.

We must understand how serious a thing it is to break God's commandments. According to God's creational design, mankind must live and the world must operate according to God's order. To violate God's commandments is to dishonor and distort the image of God within us. It is to openly blaspheme God's holy nature. It is to completely destroy the order of God's kingdom.

Man was driven out of the garden of Eden, and the path to the tree of life was guarded by cherubim. Satan enticed the ancestors of mankind, causing them to fall. They neglected the responsibility of subduing the earth that God had entrusted them with, and they strayed from God's will for his kingdom. By taking advantage of man's pride, Satan persuaded them to attempt to establish a beautiful kingdom that would make God appear superfluous. This was sin. Satan deliberately subverted the kingdom order that God had carefully designed in order to rebel against God's authority. Satan's lies not only robbed man of his authority to rule the earth, but also caused all mankind to fall under his dominion. 1 John 5:19 tells us that "the whole world lies in the power of the evil one."

The Gospel Restores Order to God's Kingdom

In Genesis 3, God curses the serpent. In the middle of this curse, he prophecies that in the future, the woman's offspring will defeat the serpent and his offspring. God wages a holy war against Satan with the intention of restoring order to his kingdom. How does he restore order to this kingdom?

Restoring order to life, to Eden, and to earth, which are all interconnected in this kingdom order, requires first that the "offspring of the woman" restore order to the disordered life of man. He must give man new life that enables him to overcome the temptations of Satan, to willingly obey God's will, and to live completely for him. Secondly, this offspring must also restore order to Eden and continually expand this order throughout this disordered world by means of man being fruitful and multiplying until order is restored to God's kingdom. In the end, this offspring will turn the whole earth into a kingdom where God dwells and rules. God will rebuild his kingdom through the gospel of Christ Jesus.

Restoring Order to Man's Life through the Incarnation of Christ

1. Christ lived as a man for the sake of men.

After mankind's first ancestors fell, no man could live out the image of God or live an ordered life. Man could no longer transform the earth into the kingdom of God by his own strength. Even though God's chosen people Israel were given a special status as royal priests, in the promised land they continued to disregard the "order of life" given to them by God. They abandoned the true God and worshiped idols. They continued to violate God's holy Law in the promised land until God finally drove them out of it.

"As it is written: 'None is righteous, no, not one; no one understands; no one seeks for God. All have turned aside; together they have become worthless; no one does good, not even one'" (Rom. 3:10–12). This means that sin has subverted the righteous, holy order of life in man so that man can no longer live out the image of God. His works have become like refuse in the eyes of God. God finds no use in them. Therefore, the Son of God, the second person of the Trinity, obeyed the will of God the Father, emptied himself, taking the form of a servant, and became a man. He willingly entered this fallen world, experienced all manner of suffering, and fulfilled the righteous requirement of the Law by living a perfect life.

The incarnation of Jesus Christ is good news because he lived as a man before God for us. John 1:4 declares, "In him was life, and the life was the light of men." His life was perfectly ordered. God gives this life to all who believe in and accept Christ. He restores the glorious image of God in them and makes them children of God. As John 1:12 promises, "But to all who did receive him, who believed in his name, he gave the right to become children of God."

2. Christ overcame temptation.

Matthew 4:1–11 says that Christ was tempted by Satan after fasting in the wilderness for forty days. Satan tempted Jesus twice with the words, "If you are the Son of God..." These words were an assault on Christ's God-given dignity and value, which is the core of the "order of life." Jesus declared that the value of his life was not found in material provisions or public affirmation but in God. Even when Jesus was tempted on the cross to save himself (Matt. 27:40), he did not allow anything in this world to define his God-given identity as God's Son. He defended the sanctity of man's God-given dignity and value and lived an ordered life. Jesus Christ overcame Satan's temptations. Adam lost the image of God, but through union with Jesus Christ God restores order to our lives.

3. Christ became a propitiatory sacrifice.

The incarnation is good news. Man rebelled against God and fell into sin. As a perfect man, Christ became a propitiatory sacrifice for men who were living under God's wrath because of their sin and saved them from judgment. When Christ Jesus came to this fallen world as a perfect man, he not only lived as a man before God for men but was offered up as a sin offering by God himself. This was how God solved the problem of man's disordered life, which man himself could never remedy. Through repentance and faith in Christ, our lives are transformed. The Holy Spirit, through a mysterious work, implants this new life purchased by Christ into the heart of man. Therefore, 2 Corinthians 5:17 declares, "If anyone is in Christ, he is a new creation."

Restoring Edenic Order through the Death and Resurrection of Christ

Christ does not only restore order to people's lives, he also establishes the Edenic order in this crooked and twisted world, an order that is distinct from the world, and places man in it.

1. The "worldly order" is under Satan's dominion.

The Bible says, "And you were dead in the trespasses and sins in which you once walked, following the course of this world, following the prince of the power of the air, the spirit that is now at work in the sons of disobedience—

among whom we all once lived in the passions of our flesh, carrying out the desires of the body and the mind, and were by nature children of wrath, like the rest of mankind" (Eph. 2:1–3). The Bible tells us that to live a disordered life is to live under the power of sin. This includes three aspects:

First, man follows "the course of this world." The world promotes a system of values that is isolated from God. It seeks meaning and satisfaction by worshiping and serving created things. Man has become used to this idolatrous lifestyle.

Second, behind the ways of this world are Satan's lies. 1 John 5:19 says, "The whole world lies in the power of the evil one." He tempts man with lies, and exercises his evil power in the lives of rebellious men (Eph. 2:2).

Third, we see that man's selfish desires are continually mixed with these lies. Man sets up the idols of the world in his own life, and these idols completely control him.

The evil power of Satan tempts man through lies to indulge in selfish desires. He establishes a "worldly order" that controls man's values and behaviors. It causes him to continually unite himself with idols. It makes him define himself according to the world. It makes him seek meaning in his selfish desires. Man has become separated from God, the giver of life. He is trapped and unable to escape.

2. Jesus Christ only worshiped and served God.

As a perfect man, Jesus Christ only worshiped and served God. When Jesus was tempted in the wilderness,

Satan offered him the world in exchange for only a little worship. This appeared to be an easy shortcut compared to how God the Father intended Christ to win the world, namely by crucifixion. But in order to serve God, Christ had to "fill the world" according to God's appointed method, according to the Edenic order. Every citizen of the garden must worship and serve God solely as priest and king. If Jesus had agreed to Satan's conditions, even if Satan had granted Jesus the authority to rule the world, this kingdom would still not have reflected God's "kingdom order." Jesus overcame Satan's temptations and faithfully served the only true God to the death. The kingdom of heaven invaded this fallen world through the gospel of Jesus Christ and began to subvert the fallen "worldly order."

3. Jesus Christ broke the power of sin through the cross.

The power of sin enslaves man through Satan's lies, the ways of the world, and man's own disordered, selfish desires. Through the truth of the gospel, Jesus Christ freed man from Satan's deceptions. Through his death on the cross, Jesus Christ thoroughly defeated Satan and fulfilled God's prophecy that said the woman's offspring would defeat the serpent and its offspring.

"I died, and behold I am alive forevermore, and I have the keys of Death and Hades" (Rev. 1:18). Through his resurrection from the dead, the Lord Jesus Christ defeated the power of death and removed its sting so that death is no longer a dreadful, hopeless thing. Jesus Christ has overcome death and the world and turns sinners into children of God. "Since therefore the children share in flesh and blood, he himself likewise partook of the same things, that through death he might destroy the one who has the power of death, that is, the devil, and deliver all those who through fear of death were subject to lifelong slavery" (Heb. 2:14–15). Christ delivers those under Satan's power from the domain of darkness and transfers them to the kingdom of the beloved Son (Col. 1:13).

4. A covenant of love has been established between Christ and his church.

The death and resurrection of Jesus Christ opened a new chapter in the life of man. Just as God created Eve from Adam's rib in the garden of Eden, Christ saved his bride, the New Testament church, through the blood and water shed from his side. The apostle Paul says, "'Therefore a man shall leave his father and mother and hold fast to his wife, and the two shall become one flesh.' This mystery is profound, and I am saying that it refers to Christ and the church" (Eph. 5:31–32). This marriage covenant depicts the sacred covenant between Christ and his church. Jesus Christ views the church as his bride. He gave his life for her and established an eternal, spiritual union with her. Christ views himself as the bridegroom. He came for his bride, that is all who truly belong to God. This is what Paul means when he says that marriage is a profound mystery. Marriage displays the covenant-keeping love and glory of Christ.

Even though Jesus's bride, the church, is not always

completely faithful to him, in this covenant the church relies on the completed work of Christ to live in the grace of God's forgiveness, justification, and promises. The church will eventually enter into that perfect unity. This amazing grace encourages the bride to joyfully rely on her husband. The church has become the new garden of Eden. God's power and abundant grace continually work within the church through Christ (Eph. 3:20), enabling it to continually operate according to the Edenic order.

5. The church is called to "be fruitful and multiply."

Jesus established the church through his resurrection from the dead, and even the power of hell cannot prevail against it (Matt. 16:18). After God created the whole earth and planted the garden of Eden, he gave man the authority to rule the earth, to "be fruitful and multiply" and to "fill the earth and subdue it." Jesus Christ won for himself all authority in heaven and on earth, and he gave this authority to the church to "make disciples of all nations." His desire is that the church would fulfill this mission of preaching the gospel throughout the whole earth (Matt. 24:14; 28:18–20).

Today, man has filled the whole earth, but he worships and serves created things rather than God. Therefore, the original command to "be fruitful and multiply" today has become a command to "make disciples of all nations." That is, through the gospel we are to make men new creations in Christ and restore order to their lives. The original command to "fill the earth"—to fill the earth with Eden—has today become a command to fill the earth with the church. The command to "subdue the earth" means that man is to exercise dominion in those areas under his jurisdiction according to God's righteousness, holiness, kindness, mercy, wisdom, and order. Today, Christians are to be light in the world. They are to live according to God's holy and righteous standards at work, in the home, and in society. They are to care for disadvantaged groups according to God's kindness and mercy. This is both a form of resistance against today's degenerate culture and a way of transforming it. Therefore, training disciples, planting churches, and renewing culture are the keys to fulfilling the mission of the church today.

Establishing Kingdom Order through the Glorious Second Coming of Christ

Jesus ultimately defeated all of his enemies through the power of his resurrection. All authority in heaven and on earth belongs to him. He will transform the whole earth into the kingdom of God. Christ will reign over this kingdom, rule in righteousness, and fully establish "kingdom order." God, through the second coming of Christ, will perfectly fulfill his original will at the beginning of creation to expand his kingdom throughout the whole earth.

In Revelation 18, God reveals to us how the great city of Babylon, which represents the civilizations of this fallen world, will finally be brought to an end. We also see how those who offered up their emotions to idols and to the great prostitute will weep, lament, and despair when Babylon falls because all they loved, all their wealth, will be lost in a moment and they will never have it again. This is the end of this fallen world.

"The kingdom of the world has become the kingdom of our Lord and of his Christ, and he shall reign forever and ever" (Rev. 11:15). When Jesus Christ returns, those of us who have been re-created in Christ, who have genuinely trusted in him in this life and served him with our lives, will rule over the new earth together with him.

Conclusion

I have offered a crude picture of the gospel by surveying the grand narrative of Scripture from the perspective of the "order of God."

The gospel presented in Scripture is kingdom-centered. The ultimate goal of Jesus is not only to save individual souls out of this fallen world but to bring the life and power of God into this material world. Christians are people who bring God's "kingdom order" into this world with the ultimate goal of completely renewing the world and restoring order to it. Now, through the crucifixion and resurrection of Christ, the kingdom of God has partially entered this world. We are now living in a time of "already but not yet." As Christians, we must live with a grand gospel vision. By the power of the Holy Spirit, we must labor in this world through the gospel and set our hope on the day when God's kingdom and power will finally come in fullness.

Brian Li

Brian Li studied at Singapore Bible College. He returned to China in 2009 and began pastoring a non-denominational evangelical house church. He is involved in church planting and marriage counseling with his wife, Stephanie, with whom he has two daughters.

Further Reflection:

- What would a gospel presentation based on the order or kingdom of God look like (as opposed to one focused on an individual's decision for Christ)? How might this apologetic be helpful for today's generation?

- What would a discipleship process based on reordering our life according to God's kingdom look like?

- How does the Creation sequence of "frame—fill—manage" help us reimagine the role of the gospel in marriage counseling, mercy and justice, church planting and more?

Endnotes

1. John Murray, *Redemption Accomplished and Applied* (Eerdmans Publishing Company, 1955), 87.

2. Anthony Hoekema, *Saved by Grace* (Grand Rapids: Eerdmans, 1989), 15.

3. Archibald Robertson, *Living Spring Greek New Testament Exegetical Notes*, vol. 6, ed. and trans. Zhan Zheng Yi (Monterey Park: Living Spring Publications), 74.

4. John Calvin, *Institutes of the Christian Religion* 3.1.1.

5. Ibid. 3.11.6.

6. Thomas Torrance, *Atonement: The Person and Work of Christ* (Downers Grove, IL: IVP Academic Press ,2009), 386.

7. Kevin DeYoung, *The Hole in Our Holiness* (Singapore: Enze Yazhou, 2012), 31.

8. Watchman Nee (Ni Tuosheng) founded the Local Church, a widespread network of independent house churches across mainland China, Taiwan, and North America. He is regarded as a martyr by many in the house church, despite the scandals which surrounded his life and ministry.

9. John Murray, *Redemption Accomplished and Applied* (Tiandao Shlou Youxian Gongsi, 1993), 127.

10. John Calvin, *Institutes of the Christian Religion* 3.2.24.

11. M. James Sawyer, *Reformed Sanctification*, http://www.mountainretreatorg.net/articles/reformed-sanctification.shtml.

12. John Calvin, *Institutes of the Christian Religion* 3.2.6.

13. Quoted in Marcus Peter Johnson, *Sanctification in Christ*, http://www.monergism.com/thethreshold/sdg/sanctification_christ.html

14. Wayne Grudem, *Biblical Doctrine*, vol. 1, God and the Bible, ed. Mai Qixin, trans. Lin Liru (Xianggang Xuesheng Fuyin Tuanqi Chubanshe, 2001), 168.

15. Michael Reeves, *Delighting in the Trinity*, 23.

16. Ibid. 24.

17. Ibid. 24-25.

18. Ibid. 26-27.

19. Ibid. 19.

20. *Baker Encyclopedia of the Bible* (simplified Chinese version), ed. Walter A. Elwell (English version) and Chen Huirong (Chinese version), trans. Gaochen Baochan, Cai Jinti (Xianggang Fuyin Zhengzhu Xiehui, 1999), 1,728.

21. Jonathan Edwards, *Religious Affections*, trans. Yang Ji (Beijing Sanlian Shudian, 2013), 125-126.

22. Yu Daxin, *Jidujiao Fazhanshi Xinyi* (Taibei Gaigezong Chubanshe, 2004), ch. 9.

23. John Owen, *Pneumatologia* (Glasgow: W. & E.

Miller, 1791), ch. 10.

24. Timothy Keller, "Biblical Change," trans. Yang Shuangmei, Church China 51 (January 2015), 32.

25. Ibid., 26.

26. Augustine, *Confessions* 1.1.

27. *The Westminster Shorter Catechism*, Question 1.

28. Michael Reeves, *Delighting in the Trinity*, 60.

29. R.C. Sproul, *At Stake: The Gospel*, introduction to *Are We Together?: A Protestant Analyzes Roman Catholicism* (Reformation Trust Publishing, 2012), 1.

30. D.A. Carson, "What Is the Gospel? –Revisited," in For the Fame of God's Name: Essays in Honor of John Piper, ed. Sam Storms and Justin Taylor (Wheaton, Ill.: Crossway, 2010), 158.

31. The author here is referring to Pastor Wang Yi (王怡), who was imprisoned in December, 2018, and sentenced to nine years in prison for "inciting to subvert state power."

32. D.A. Carson, *The Biblical Gospel*, trans. Shu Ning, prf. Xu, Church China 50, no. 6 (November 2014), 21.

33. The author is referring to a paper by S.E. Wang, Gospel Theology and Cross Theology, Church China 56, no. 6 (November 2015), 3.

34. Timothy Keller, *Center Church*, 32.

35. Ibid.

36. See Timothy Keller, "The Centrality of the Gospel," 2000. Accessed at gospelinlife.com.

37. Geerhardus Vos, *Redemptive History and Biblical*

Interpretation: The Shorter Writings of Geerhardus Vos, ed. R.B. Gaffin, Jr. (Phillipsburg, NJ: P&R Publishing, 2001), 231–232.

38. Leon Morris, *The Cross in the New Testament*, trans. Li Lijuan (Beijing: Zongjiao Wenhua Chubanshe, 2013), 276.

39. John Piper, *The Legacy of Sovereign Joy*, trans. Du Hua (Shanghai Zhongxi Shuju, 2012), 1.

40. Douglas J. Moo, *The Letter to the Romans*, trans. Cheng Zhi (Meiguo Maizhong Chuandaohui, 2012), 39.

41. Timothy Keller, *Preaching: Communicating Faith in an Age of Skepticism*, trans. Zheng Chunyi (Xinbei: Xiaoyuan Shufang, 2018), 50-51.

42. Carl Trueman, *Luther on the Christian Life: Cross and Freedom*, trans. Wang Yi (Shanghai Sanlian Shudian, 2019), 110.

43. Cornelius Plantinga, *Engaging God's World* (Eerdmans, 2002), 103-104, 137-138.

About the Editors

Qiangwei is a former house church pastor in a major Chinese city. She currently serves through writing and editing in order to help develop the house church's future writers and thinkers.

Hannah Nation is a graduate of Covenant College and received her Master of Arts in Church History from Gordon-Conwell Theological Seminary. As a student of global Christianity, she is inspired by this historical moment and the privilege of witnessing a new chapter in church history unfold across China. Nation currently serves as the Managing Director of the Center for House Church Theology and as Content Director for China Partnership. She is a research associate at Gordon-Conwell's Center for the Study of Global Christianity and has written for The Gospel Coalition, Christianity Today, byFaith Magazine, and the World Christianity Encyclopedia.

This book was made possible in part by the generous support of our partners, who have walked with us through twenty years of serving, training, and resourcing the Chinese church together. Thank you for helping the gospel go deeper and wider in China so that the whole world may reap the fruit of God's faithfulness in the Middle Kingdom.

To find out how you can partner with us in praying for, encouraging, and learning from the church in China, follow us at chinapartnership.org

CHINA PARTNERSHIP

Made in the USA
Columbia, SC
21 October 2021

47196026R10074